Doing Big and Scary!
London to Paris the Hard Way

By Andy Mouncey

14, Croydon Road, Waddon,
Croydon, Surrey CR0 4PA
+44 (0)208 688 2598
Fax +44 (0)208 774 9913
sales@filamentpublishing.com

Printed by Antony Rowe Ltd, Chippenham & Eastbourne
Design & Layout Charlotte Mouncey
Photography Timothy Jury

ISBN 0 - 9546531 - 5 - 7

For those who believed.
And for those who did not.

But most of all for Charly.
For everything.

Contents

In The Beginning...

In the mid-1980's the first London to Paris Triathlon relay was completed by a team of four, and since then the two cities have been linked every so often by triathlon teams of various sizes - each team member taking turns to run, swim and cycle a few miles in turn.

In 2001 Englishman Eddie Ette became the first person to complete a solo continuous crossing between London and Paris using the three triathlon disciplines establishing a World Record mark of 80 hours 5 minutes. The Enduroman Arch to Arc challenge was pioneered by Eddie over some 3 years and is owned by his company, Enduroman. It comprises an 87 mile run from Marble Arch to Dover, a 22 mile swim across the English Channel and a 187 mile cycle ride from Calais to the Arc De Triomphe, Paris. The clock starts in London and stops in Paris: rest and delays due to bad weather over the Channel, for instance, all count towards the final cumulative time.

The challenge - weather permitting - is to complete all three stages as close together as possible - on your own!

Pretty Big & Scary stuff, huh?

That's what I thought when I met Eddie in September 2002 and heard about it for the first time. I was in Portland, Dorset for the Chesil Challenge, a multisport weekend which Ed was staging for idiots like me looking for a slightly different... 'personal challenge.' I'd been in this triathlon game since the mid-1980s, and with a few ironman distance races under my belt, (2.4 mile swim, 112 miles on the bike, then run a marathon) I was definitely looking for something... slightly different. Eddie's idea of a short swim was 8 miles - and as the only other option was the 'long' 17 miler - I said 'what the hell' and got on with 8 miles.

Let's just say it was an illuminating experience.

But the seed was sown and it grew on me over the winter and New Year. A few phone calls to Portland to test the water till finally in February, I sat Charlotte, my wife, down one evening and announced, "I've been thinking...!" She looked straight at me, paused and replied, "Okayyyyy- just let me get back to you on that one, will you!"

And a few nights later she did. "Tell me why, then."

Fortunately I had most of it rehearsed. The chance to shoot for a World Record. Only the second time it will have been done - ever, how cool would that be! The current Record Holder is prepared to help me - now that's GOT to be worth something! And what an opportunity! This chance may never come again - we have no kids so why not now? And if we can do this - what else could we do in the future? In terms of my business I can do it - put a line through my diary if I want. OK it'll be tough - real tough, and I'd have to commit to the preparation big-style - but I can do COMMIT and I can do perseverance like you wouldn't believe. Bloody hell, I started my own business 3 years ago and THAT'S not been easy either!

But here's the real clincher: I'm a Performance Coach - my business is helping people do Big & Scary stuff. Now I admire integrity in myself and others - the Mouth and Trouser Test, I call it... and we all know people who are all mouth and no trousers! So if I'm any good as a Coach I ought to be able to apply them to myself. My specialist sport is triathlon, so let's take the Biggest & Scariest triathlon I can find, and use it as a bloody great field test for my coaching! Pretty powerful stuff for the business if it comes off, huh?

But I want you with me on this one babe so we do it together or not at all.

My dear wife however, is a bit smarter than that. 'Let me think on it for a few days, will you?' Completely understandable as I'm pretty sure I hit her with this not long after she came in from work. I'd been working on this since before Xmas: only fair to let her do a bit of catching up!

So I did Patient Husband for a few days.

"Here's the deal," said Charly a little later. "Two things, if we do this I'm not living with a basket-case for 4 months while you get yourself in shape. We have to have some balance and I have to have some stuff to look forward to that WE can do together. We plan in the quality time NOW otherwise it will be too late when we need it."

Fair one. And the second thing?

"I want to meet Eddie" she said. "We go down to Portland, we talk, we meet his friends, we be absolutely clear that this guy is for real and this thing will work."

It all sounds good so far, but my wife hasn't quite finished yet.

"There is just one other thing though…"

Is that a rock I can see heading straight for me?

"I want to meet his wife."

Part One
Getting Ready

"Tell me, who has ever been prepared when starting anything off from scratch? You have to learn, experience, battle against problems that occur. The trouble is that when things don't go your way in the first year, 99% of people just give up, rather than tweaking a bit here, changing a bit there to get a better result. Our first two years were terrible."

Julian Metcalf on launching the Pret A Manger chain.

1
Taking A Deep Breath

Saturday, 24th May 2003

I'm in Portland chez Eddie for what I know will be a weekend of getting intimate with the ocean and for Eddie to size me up. While he knows my results from Chesil Challenge last year, he has not actually seen me swim and we are still finding out about how the other ticks. Getting to know each other well will be vital for the attempt - as much as the physical preparation.

It all starts here...

I will be coming down here every 2 weeks from now on for the simple purpose of getting myself into Channel swim shape specifically, and Arch shape generally.

Charlotte is down with me so she can see for herself just what this whole thing entails. She knows this whole endurance sport bit pretty well by now, but we both recognise this is a very different gig, and I do this with her support or not at all.

So after 6 hours of battling bank holiday traffic, it's 4pm and we're drinking tea with Eddie. 'What's the plan, then?' I ask. 'Let's just chuck you in the water and see what happens,' replies The Man Who Has Done It All Before, 'You want to go lumpy or calm?' ' Lumpy' I reply. 'Right, Chesil it is then.'

Lyme Bay, Chesil Beach is indeed 'lumpy' and I know it will be cold. I have no idea how long this will be, but I do know that Eddie is watching and Charlotte is a mite nervous...

Just shy of an hour later I stagger up the beach shaken, chilled and definitely stirred! It's been rough and cold despite a full wetsuit; I wrestled driftwood, seaweed, plastic bags and definitely tasted Mother Nature BUT Eddie has seen what he wants and I've got the first one out of the way and feel MUCH happier!

After sampling the local fish - cooked this time - and hospitality, it's off to bed in preparation for the morrow.

Sunday, 25th May

The boat slowly chugs out of Weymouth harbour as Wendy and I get ready to swim. She is preparing to swim the Channel in July - and for that they definitely don't allow you to wear wetsuits or big woolly hats. Wendy has a 3-4 hour session today and my total respect.

Tom Watch guides the boat round. He is Mr Channel Swim in these parts: has guided Eddie and numerous other folks to successful swims and what he doesn't know about open water swimming isn't worth talking about. I know I am in great hands, but also under scrutiny. Tom and Ed need to see stuff today that in their view will enable me to get across. The plan is simple: 'we're going to swim you till you drop' said Eddie. I have no idea what that will mean, but I have 2 hours in my head. Eddie's wife Lynne is also with us: she completed her own successful Channel crossing last year and will keep Wendy company for her last 2 hours today.

My first feed and that means 45 mins. So far so good in air temp 54 degrees and water 56 degrees and it's relatively calm. I'm definitely not warm but everything's working and the stroke rate is staying around 63.

80 mins and the cold is starting to bite. I'm starting to shiver and slow as the rate drops. The second feed comes 50 mins after the first. I say nothing and just focus on the essentials...

Now it's really going pear-shaped: shaking has set in all through the body and I'm perfecting the art of swimming with clenched teeth. I stop frequently (which is bad) hear Ed and Tom shouting (which is good) but strangely enough screaming in frustration and cold at the sea while treading water doesn't seem to help.

"15 minutes!" comes the shout. I know I can do 15 minutes, can't I? I wouldn't call it swimming but my arms are moving and I'm still in the water so it must be. Something hard hits me: that'll be the boat then... "2 minutes, Andy!! 2 minutes!!" and I know I can do 2 minutes, so I get my head down and force my arms around at the prospect of finally stopping and getting out of this freezer.

Sitting in the boat with all my clothes on while the sun shines trying unsuccessfully to keep coffee in the cup as my body behaves as though someone is shoving a few thousand volts through it.

It was important to do 2 hours: I'm pleased and Ed and Tom are encouraging while we compare notes. "You're never as cold as you think you are," notes Tom "I reckon you had another 20-30 minutes before it got really serious." That sobers me up. Of all the lessons here this is probably the biggest. To stop the cold I need to keep the work rate high. That includes fitness, brief and more frequent feeds, and overridding the brain's signals. Should be simple then... ✕ A big watershed, nevertheless and I dedicate the rest of the day to warmth..!

Monday, 26th May

8am and I'm once more ploughing the surf off the Chesil side with Eddie and Charlotte in coach and coastguard role on the beach. The sea is calmer and it feels a little easier already... 30 minutes along the shoreline and Eddie calls me into the beach. "OK, take it back harder will you?" Sure thing. I switch the breathing to every left stroke, get my head down and up the stroke rate to 65 for the return trip. It really is a lovely morning - though the water feels colder this time - and I seem to have recovered from yesterday's frolics. 'Finger, wrist, elbow' goes the mantra as I work to iron out the braking effect a dropped elbow has during the power phase, but it is a good deal faster on the return trip and there are smiles all round.

A quick breakfast and we are heading back up to Leicestershire after 3 very valuable days (and 2 tired shoulders) from which we have learnt much and will try differently next time.

Tuesday, 27th May - Sunday, 1st June
The first big week as physical and organisational preparation has kicked in. My usual 2-3 swims a week has doubled and then some, so the ole upper body has been asking questions which so far the brain is able to answer! The running is solid - my strength - and this will just get better very quickly. I am keeping everything very steady for the first part of the build up. The only quality training is in the pool and in the weights room.

My priority is the swimming, and I don't want to be trashing my self with the other two so that I am stuffed in the water. (There is also the small matter of working for a living, and as a self employed dude the equation is quite simple: I don't earn, I go hungry...) The addition of regular cold water baths has helped recovery as well as acclimatisation and worryingly I am starting to look forward the sound of running cold water in the house...

The wetsuit is in for an MOT and various cold water survival goodies are on order. I am even considering venturing into our local lake sans suit, which is either a sign of building confidence or sheer bloody minded focus!

The niggle is the bike at the moment. In my mind this is the least important part of the challenge - (get me across the Channel and just make me stay on my trusty steed all the way into Paris even if it takes me a week) - so it's way down the list at the moment. I'm messing with my sexy bike set up which is still frustrating me. It's been a while since I rode it full aero in anger as I've reverted to a more relaxed road set up. I've also been off the bike since mid April so I know it will take a few weeks to start to feel close to good again. Patience and perseverance. I'm not planning to bring it all to the boil at the same time anyway, and I know what to do to ride well enough to do the job!

We are starting to let a few folks know about the attempt - not least as I am finalising the launch press release and sponsorship shopping list. Reactions have been interesting and range from absolute bafflement and disbelief to full cheerleader stuff. It's easy to forget that when Charly and I are in our Dorset base, we are surrounded by people who understand the commitment, are fully supportive and believe I can do this thing. Come away from there and it is a very different story! This really hit home when it quickly became obvious that a couple of close friends really thought I'd not a cat in hells chance. They didn't say it, but I knew... Now I don't normally get off on proving folks wrong, but I might just consider it in this case..!

Rest day and massage tomorrow: bring it on!

2
One Swim Too Far

Tuesday, 3rd - Thursday, 5th June

A busy few days earning a crust and getting launch details and press releases out and starting to talk to some keys folks in my network about raising the profile (and some funds!) for this wee jaunt. We won't starve over the next three months, but I am deliberately NOT chasing new business - just making sure I have enough to tick over. The usual Wednesday and Thursday sessions were all managed, then it was time to get ready for three days in Dorset once again.

Friday, 6th June

Four hours in the car saw me in Portland for 10am. It's blowing a gale and raining - not too bad for yours truly who will be IN the sea, but definitely bad news for Ed who will be ON it accompanying me in the canoe!

The good news is that the water is about 2 degrees warmer than my last foray, and I am armed with earplugs and neoprene socks for additional heat retention! "2 hours" declares Eddie, as he readies a fishing line to trawl from the canoe, "and we'll see if we can catch tea as well!" Impressive multi-tasking...

Now I know 2 hours damn well near finished me last time, but I am up for this and have learned from my last trip. We head out from the base and parallel the causeway towards Weymouth. First feed of a warm carb drink at 35 minutes and everything feels good. We are close into the lee of the land so are protected from the worst of the weather. I focus on a relaxed rhythm breathing every third stroke. Successfully avoiding a posse of windsurfers the second feed comes at 70 minutes with an additional energy gel which I am testing. We are heading back into the wind and swell, but my stroke feel better and the rate remains high. I also feel much warmer - though it is all relative!

It's an all round much better swim as we land in just under 2 hours. I'm grinning and shivering as we both head up the ramp - sadly with no fish for tea though - and into the base for the welcome hot shower.

Tomorrow we have two 2 hour swims planned which is quite a test, though later that evening when Charlotte and I talk on the phone she is very upbeat about the day and the prospects for tomorrow. This is all good stuff, and I go to bed with one of my favourite quotations running round my brain:

'You must do that which you think you cannot.'

Saturday, 7th June

Slept well and awake before 6am. A lighter breakfast this time - still trying to find a formula which means I can eat and get thrown around in the sea and drink seawater AND keep food where it should be... if you gotta go, you gotta go - and wearing a wetsuit is just all part of the experience!

Lynne (Mrs Ette) is on coach duty this morning, and she will walk the beach with me and be a provider of sustenance and Chief Cheerleader. Half past eight and I'm ploughing up the shoreline in Weymouth Bay reacquainting myself with the resident spider crabs some 2 metres below me: I get the feeling I'll be on first name terms with some of those guys before the end of August!

It's warmer but overcast. I'm so comfortable that at the first feed I ditch the socks: MISTAKE! All is not so rosy 35 minutes later and I replace them! Although the last third of the swim is in the roughest water, my stroke count stays in the mid-60s and I finish pretty much in control. One down...

Some food and a short sleep later it is just after 2pm and I'm squeezing myself into a damp wetsuit - assisted by copious amounts of talcum powder - once again at the start point on Weymouth Bay. We will repeat the course of the morning swim, though this time it is Ed on duty as Lynne is heading into the water with me. I know the second hour will be the test, so focus hard on keeping relaxed through the water and the first two feeds pass fairly comfortably. Ed has given me landmarks to swim to, but because I am uncertain as to exactly where I'm going, (and because I am willing the distance away) I'm sighting and checking with Ed way too much. Ed says afterwards he thought I might be getting ready to pack it in. I'm not, but I should just trust Ed and get my head down and swim - not least because I stay warmer that way!

Once again the last quarter is a fight into the swell and wind. I am joined by Tom in the boat who has been helping with a swim elsewhere in the Bay. He has come to check the progress of the shell of a bloke he fished out of the Bay two weeks ago. With about 10 minutes to go my arms and shoulders finally pack in, but it's not bad timing at all. I'm bushed and definitely colder than this morning - but am delighted to complete my second two hour swim of the day! This was the Big One, and I am grinning stupidly through the shivers...

We talk about tomorrow as we get showered and warm. Ed wants to go for 3 hours. I definitely don't. In my mind, I have achieved what I set out to do this weekend and demonstrated big progress on 2 weeks ago: I don't NEED 3 hours tomorrow. I am happy, but contemplating hauling my ass through cold water again to the point of clenched teeth is rapidly deflating me. I talk to Ed. 'OK' he says 'Let's take it to 2 hours and see...' It's not really what I want to hear, but I settle for it and start to focus on more pressing matters like eating as much as I can in the next hour or so...

Sunday, 8th June

I wake tired, stiff and depressed. It's a lovely morning but I really don't want this swim! Still, I pick myself up and get body and mind ready, and by the time we are chugging in the boat to the start point I've convinced myself this will be OK if I take it a bit at a time. However, the cover job doesn't fool everyone, and Lynne tells me later she KNEW I wasn't a happy bunny! The Bay is windy and quite rough, but I actually enjoy this first bit as we swim towards sheltered water along the harbour arms. Wendy is with me - wanting a mere 2 hours after a 6 hour swim earlier in the week.

Feed number 2. I want to stop. No, really. I've been pissing about for the last 15 mins because I am just not into this - I just don't NEED to be here, dammit and it's another boring, wet, cold shit-arsed sea which I did to death yesterday, didn't I? So as a consequence I am cold, and to add injury to insult my suit is rubbing in areas it has never rubbed before. I tell Eddie but he stonewalls. He knows I'm physically OK because my stroke isn't falling apart. I expect the ladder to come down over the side any second, but he's smarter than that "You'll regret it if you get out now" I pause. Bollocks. It's not going to happen, is it.

Eventually I swim on, but it's an awful parody of my usual stroke as my brain goes walkabout. Ed simply keeps the boat 30 yards away from me and heckles "You've got 15 minutes if you stay still like that or 7 minutes if you swim to the end. Your choice." I'm back to swimming with the shakes so he's right - I have to swim on, and I can do 7 minutes, can't I? Some time later I look up and the ladder is over the side of the boat. I am beyond feelings now, but Ed saves the best till last "Swim another 6 minutes and you've got 2 hours - 6 minutes, that's all! Come on, Andy, show us what you've got - 6 minutes!" Fuck it. I let go of the ladder and drop back into the welcoming cold for the final embrace…

And the lessons? Well, there's a few and some old favourites from 2 weeks ago:

- I simply have to be able do this even when I don't want to.
- There is very little sensory stimulus in open water swimming - so either create some or accept it and get on with it!
- I am never as cold as I think I am.
- Play to the whistle (!)
- I must do that which I think I cannot…

Tom and Ed are delighted but I'm too mentally fried to reciprocate too much. This mood persists and it is only 3 days later that I am able to reflect honestly. I could and should have nailed that 2 hours. This is not a choice thing. I know that if I want to stand any chance of getting across I HAVE to commit to every aspect of the swim preparation and to trust the folks around me. It was a massive weekend for progress, and I AM delighted. If I can make that much progress in a short time then chances just get better and better - so let's stop being a drama queen, shall we?!?

3
Starting To Adjust

Monday, 9th - Sunday, 15th June

No training Monday or Tuesday, just a well deserved massage, as busy with work and mentally a little frazzled! I spend time reviewing the last three weeks on Tuesday, but it takes me till Wednesday to feel good about Sunday's effort.

It's clear at the moment that the Portland weekends are all about the big swims. I need all my energies for these so any other training will just detract from my swim performance. I want to build other sessions into these visits, but I now know I am going to have to do this much more gradually than first envisaged.

I have another look at training structure for the next 12 weeks. The first 6 weeks will be base conditioning with some strength work, followed by a block of 5 weeks with some quality introduced, finished off with a final block of over-distance work. To be honest, I am still experimenting and expect this to evolve again. The one solid element is that the investment in the swimming is already starting to pay off and I HAVE to keep this as the central theme. I believe the next most important element is the run, and although this is my strength, I want to be able to do this well but get to Dover comfortably. I must let the bike go as the reality is that I have only so much energy to give - and I still need to run my business during this preparation period. I know from past experience that specific strength training will help me to complete the run and ride sections without huge training volumes, so I need to work these in much more over the next few weeks.

I keep the sessions short and varied for the rest of the week, but get wiped out Friday with hayfever.

It's a pretty big week travelling for work. While the longer term looks good for my business, I feel I have the right irons in the right fires and some are starting to glow nicely. The short term is pretty pants! The simple fact is that I need to earn, and though I've learned not to be freaked out by a diary empty of appointments, it remains a great way to concentrate the mind!

As word is now starting to filter out about the Attempt, I am starting to get some nibbles on the support / sponsorship front - all of which is very welcome as I have yet to really drive this. My strategy is two-fold to focus on people and organisations I have helped over the last 2 years or so and to find businesses with an English - French connection. A key will be the amount and quality of media coverage we can secure, so I am starting to explore this through the contacts I have. I know this whole aspect will be a product of repeat contacts and perseverance. This stuff rarely comes off after one hit. Let's face it - who buys anything new after seeing it only once?

Ed calls on Friday, "Can you get down here on Monday as it looks like the weather will break after that?" A subsequent re-jig of the diary means that I will travel down Sunday night for a Big Swim Monday. "Any thoughts on what you want to do?" asks Eddie. Nice pass! "It has to be 3, doesn't it" I reply, "and I'm up for it so let's do it!' 'Good man!" comes the chuckle from the other end of the phone, "3 hours it is!"

Monday, 16th June

7am in the Ette household and The Man and I are multi-tasking with a vengeance: shovelling porridge in and business planning between mouthfuls! It's that Big and Scary thing again rearing it's head, a new venture with time, energy, money, blood, sweat and tears invested and not as much to show for it as you want. It's timely to re-visit part of the WHY we are both doing this, to help each others' businesses, and for Ed it's very simple - there needs to be life after my September Attempt, as this is simply a showcase for *Enduroman...*

It's a beautiful morning and we're down on the boat for 9am once again with Wendy who is gearing up for her big 10 hour test later this week. Tom is in ' now let's stop ****ing about' mode and the message is in characteristically blunt Tom-speak, it's going to be cold so get used to it as it's all in the head. He nevertheless fails to dent the buoyant mood in the boat. It's a Monday morning, glorious weather, and we're out on the sea when most people are at work. A three hour swim? Bring it on! So while Wendy shares her new purchase with Ed and Tom, (lubricant normally used for cows' udders - but apparently it does a great job for Channel swimmers as well) I don my usual gear and head off into a practically flat calm bay.

Weymouth Bay, look no waves!

The stroke feels smooth and I'm breathing comfortably every 3 strokes while working to keep the elbows high. The first feed takes ages to arrive as usual, but the second is faster and then they just arrive by magic! Wendy gets in after about an hour which gives me another body to key off in the water. I go through periods of cold and shaking but the big difference this time is that I just swim through them. My mental state is SO different from my last outing. I experiment with passing the time by counting up to 100 strokes repeatedly - well, if it works for Paula Radcliffe...but as I periodically vary the breathing I find it difficult to keep track.

The wind and swell gets up on the return trip, but it's still OK and for the first time I lose track of time: I think I'm at 2 hours 40 mins when I'm actually at 3 hours. Hell, let's just do this thing! Tom and Ed are really encouraging as it's obvious I'm OK, so a cup of tea later I'm off for a wee bit more. I start to struggle after another 20 mins as cramps affect my guts again, though it's no where near as bad as previous, and my back and shoulders really start to tighten.

I call a halt at 3 hours 45 mins DELIGHTED that it is fatigue which has stopped me and not cold this time! We're all happy bunnies. In Tom's words I'm a third of the way across (the Channel distance) and there are 12 weeks to go.

4
Focus On What You Can Control

Tuesday, 17th - Sunday, 22nd June

And then it all went a bit pants as I launched myself into a work frenzy for the next few days for all the WRONG reasons! With little paying work booked in and uncertainty about my biggest earner I went into stressed-and-scared-rabbit-in-headlights mode. Really helpful. Charly was certainly wondering what just happened as I did Scary and Short Fuse Husband for a while!

Equilibrium returns pretty quickly though. We are a team and we will find a way to make it work as we always have done. Discipline and quality training resume by Thursday. I scribble this in my diary:

' *You've made a commitment: A World Record for Chrissake!! Quit bellyaching and take the opportunity. Remember you have the love of a beautiful woman AND her support - so pull her close DON'T push her away. Slow down. Enjoy the challenge.*'

Monday, 23rd - Thursday, 26th June

A busy time work-wise at the start of the week meant little training, but I have learned to view this as good physical rest time so I concentrate on fewer but longer stints of training rather than a little every day. This is an approach which goes back to my Ironman triathlon preparation where I focused on 3 big sessions over a 7 day period, and anything else was a bonus.

The big uncertainty work-wise remains with British Swimming, my biggest monthly earner. It all rather comes to a head towards the end of the week, (and I could write a book about that one as well!). Much phone and email time later, it appears that I will become yet another victim of politics and spending cuts which means that 'my' athletes may be facing changing their coach a year out from the Olympics. Well, it clearly makes sense to someone! This will run for a wee while yet though... 'Uncertainty', the greatest nightmare for us self-employed folks!

Friday, 27th June

Portland 10.30am. "So, what's on your mind for this weekend?" asks Ed. "A 2 and a 4 and a half" I reply. Wrong answer: Eddie shakes his head and looks away. "It has to be 5. It has to be. There's no point pissing about with little progressions - we HAVE to get up there as quickly as we can - you only have 7 big swims left and we need to do a couple of 6's, an 8 and a 10."

Ed warms to his theme, "I wish you had seen Wendy do her 10 hours last week - it just hit me: BANG! The difference between the two of you - how much you still have to do."

Hmm, doing the 'bad cop' routine this morning then? This is not going to phase me and I need to bring this back to a focus on MY progress as right now I can't even contemplate 10 hours. "Yeah, but look how far I've come already. I'm really pleased with that 'cos we've made big strides every time we've gone out."

I smile inside as Ed continues to talk about Wendy's swim. He is understandably proud of her achievement, but this line of conversation is straight out of the coaching manual. How to make Big and Scary appear even more Big and Scary and consequently it is definitely not helpful to me at the moment!

"She was practically asleep at one stage, her stroke rate dropped right off - but after we stopped and fed her she got right back into it. Her endurance base is awesome... what really has me worried is that last time it wasn't the cold which stopped you, it was fatigue."

Fair one, but I bring it back again: "Yeah, I know, but I'm making huge progress and every time we're out I'm building - last time I doubled it. It'll come, I know it - and we'll soon know if it's my base as it will show in the 5 hour."

We've set ourselves a very ambitious target over a short timescale, and I really only now understand how ambitious it is. This is quite simply the hardest physical thing I've ever done.

I have understood from the very start that I have a choice about how I stay sane during the preparation. I can look at what I still have to do, (and be very scared!) or I can look at how far I have come in a short period, (and draw confidence from this). No prizes for guessing which approach I'm adopting. While it's appropriate to look over the fence every now and again and I understand that comparisons will be made between me and others, I CANNOT dwell on this and HAVE to turn it to my favour when it happens.

'You must do that which you think you cannot.' Absolutely - just try not to get too spooked in the process!

On the 'doing' front, I put away a 2 hour swim across Portland Harbour to the breakwater on the North Ship Canal and back with Ed tracking me in his canoe with no problems. (We now do a 2 hour session just to 'stretch out' - interesting how the boundaries move, isn't it?).

I plan on running later, so some food, a short sleep and I'm out for 90 minutes exploring the paths around Portland on a glorious late afternoon. The views are just breathtaking, and I'm truly glad to be on this earth!

Saturday, 28th June - Big Swim Day

There's definitely a feeling of butterflies in my stomach as I drive down to Boscowan Pool to meet Eddie. I've been up since 6am, a lighter than normal breakfast of porridge, banana and then an energy bar an hour later as I'm still experimenting with ways to keep the calories inside… Lying on the bed relaxing and thinking good thoughts about the swim, remember 'nerves are good…'

It's another beautiful morning with light winds. You wouldn't think a sunny day would make much of a difference when you're ploughing along with the fish - believe me, it makes HEAPS! I try hard not to think Big Picture. Today I have to swim further than I've ever swum before and to add at least 75 minutes to my last effort. Pretty soon I'll be so far out of my comfort zone I'll need a telescope to look back and see it…

Ed and I will do the first one and a half hours or so together - with Ed in the canoe - before meeting Tom and the boat just off the Weymouth Harbour mouth. It's a way of getting started early and I want to get this thing done. Just relax for the first 2 hours and take it from there…

The initial short easy strokes get me quickly into the groove. I'm swimming straighter than yesterday but still focus on the pitch of my hands in the water. It's calm in the harbour and all is in the green. We're feeding as usual but the first cold spell comes earlier than previously this time. No panic, just swim through. Out in the Bay and it's definitely rougher. I know we're dog-legging as Ed waits to spot Tom. A few weeks ago this would have driven me mad, but I'm now more disciplined, trust my support more and understand that the best thing I can do is to keep my head down and swim. It really doesn't make a difference where I am!

"Pick the stroke rate up!" shouts Eddie, "You'll get cold if you don't." He's right, I've gone to sleep a bit, so visualising dustbin lids on my hands as huge paddles - yes, really! - I up the rate and quickly feel good ploughing down the bay.

The familiar shape of Tom's boat comes into view - does that mean we're at about 2 hours? - and Ed quickly secures the canoe and climbs aboard. I get a thumbs up as the usual routine resumes. It's definitely bumpy out here with a combination of swell, wind and pleasure boats. I'm still doing the dustbin lid bit and enjoying the manufactured sensation of pulling myself along with huge handfuls of water. Hey - whatever works!

First feed at the boat and I start on the solids. I've now perfected my 'boat hanging' routine which goes like this. Swim to the bow of the boat and let the boat come to me. Hand onto the gunwale lie back and let my legs float under the keel. Goggles up and noseclip off and hand to crew. Make eye contact, feed with one hand, listen, talk and look around. Today's treat is fruit cake washed down by warm energy drink as Tom and I exchange morning greetings.

A 180 degree turn in the middle of Weymouth Bay means we're heading back to Portland Harbour entrance, and then I know it's less than an hour in a straight line back to the base in what I hope will be calmer water. I can definitely do this and focus on keeping my head down and simply swimming through the chop.

I'm feeling sore and the suit is starting to rub at the next feed. Tom dissolves some painkillers and hands me the cup. I don't really have time to consider the ethics of this and swill it down like a good boy.

A final test is still to come however...

Back at the harbour entrance Ed and Tom hand me the feed. 'We're going to head down the breakwater and along the shore for a bit'. My spirits sink, obviously not straight back then, and to make it even more interesting it's definitely not calm in here. I know it's pointless saying anything, so I do 'Stoic' and get on with the job - but my stroke rate drops right off as my swimming matches my mood. My slow progress means I'm swallowing more water which also means I'm starting to feel sick - and then I start to stop and look around...

NOT good, but I'm fed up now and want to finish. We are in a straight line to the base, but funnily enough it's not getting closer! Even passing through a flotilla of windsurfers and dingies doesn't phase me as my universe is slowly contracting around me! Then Ed calls me in, "That's it, you've done it" I'm a little slow with my comprehension so Ed has to repeat it. 'That's 5 hours -so it's up to you now, you can get out or continue for as far as you can." There's a long pause. I'm heartily sick of salt water, I can feel my suit burns... but I know the main problem is that I'm just feeling a bit sorry for myself. "OK, I'll see how far I can get." Right idea, but 10 minutes later I really have finished for good, and the welcome sight of the ladder at the side of the boat signals 'game over' for the day.

I've added nearly a hour and a half to my previous best. I'm not too cold, and while I am tired it is much more the 'glad it's over' feeling which dominates. As I try to explain to people when they ask, I can't say it's fun, but it is something I simply have to do. The satisfaction and reward comes from completing the thing and pushing further each time I'm out. So I just sit quietly in the boat for a few minutes and let the 'job well done' feelings surface while Tom and Ed offer their own congratulations. Smiles all round as I look the few hundred yards to the shore... I could have swum that, couldn't I?!

Sunday, 29th June
A well deserved day of rest

5
Wobbles

Monday, 30th June - Saturday, 5th July

It all went a bit pearshaped this week. Definitely feeling flat at the start of the week with all my usual mental and physical signs telling me all is not well. I am sleeping poorly and wasting time by distracting myself with non-work / Arch stuff. I've also picked up some really nice burns from the wetsuit right in the crook of the arms which will be difficult to heal quickly. There is no point continuing to swim - I need to let these heal otherwise I will be in trouble repeatedly during future big swims. I get a big break work-wise Tuesday which lifts the morale, but I don't train till Wednesday, and then it all goes black again on Thursday. I write in my diary:

'No training - again! Slept very poorly: awake in the early hours just being a stress-head! Feeling out of control and small and scared. I want to be a good husband. I've taken on some new work I probably shouldn't have. The continuing uncertainty with my British Swimming work is getting to me - it's looking increasingly likely it will cease. I need consistency in training and have allowed this week to throw me. Still trying to parcel work up to leave me with big training hits. Doing this solo is proving real tough...'

Charly finds herself doing an impromptu session of Husband-Counselling at 7.30am in the morning when I announce that I don't want to do the Big Swim this weekend - she moans that no one at work will believe her when she comes in late for work. They all think we're some kind of Super-Couple!

The talking helps as I remember why we work so well together, and why this thing is important for both of us. We decide to go to Dorset later than planned but to do the 10 mile swim on Sunday, Charlotte being adamant that she is not going to miss a chance to go in the support boat particularly as the forecast is good!

Normal service resumes on Friday, the first time all week I've felt half decent.

Start of the Weymouth to Lulworth. Big Merv (Local Channel swimming veteran) on Start Duty - Betcha he doesn't wear a girlie wetsuit.

Sunday, 6th July - Weymouth to Lulworth Cove 10 mile race

7.30am and I'm greasing up on Weymouth Pier. Normally I charge for this but there's really very few people interested at this time of day..! I'm with seven other swimmers from the local area taking part in the resurrection of this race which has been a part of the local calendar for many years, but not recently. At least half those present are Channel veterans, so we're in good company.

It's a beautiful morning and the sea is flat calm. The swim will simply follow the Dorset Heritage Coast 10 miles east and we are told that the water and the view will be quite special in places. I'm relaxed and looking forward to having Charly in the support boat for company... and for the first 3.5 hours or so it does all go really well. I'm cruising along quite comfortably enjoying being in some uncharted waters. The chalk cliffs to my left really are quite stunning and my competitive juices are starting to rise as I realise I am gaining on Kate in second place. Then the wheels start to come off.

Some warning signs have been there. It's my old favourite loose bowels again pretty much after the first hour or so and, without going into the clinical detail too much, sometimes I've caught it and sometimes I haven't. By three hours, my muscles in my torso are spasming and this has spread to my lower back, hips and hamstrings. I start to slow which means that of course I get colder, and then I'm losing interest in the whole damn thing.

Charly holds a bottle up signalling feed-time. I swim in and hang off the boat so I'm flat on my back in the water trying to ease the cramp in the muscles. If I clench my jaw any more I'll need a visit to the dentist after this. It's not pleasant for either of us and I'm avoiding eye contact for lots of reasons - not least that I'm ashamed. I look despairing down the coast and ask the stupid question; "How far?' Charly and Paul (who is piloting the boat) point ahead and say something about not being far. It's not enough for me. "Where?" I grit my teeth and try and find a landmark to fix on. Charly decides to fight fire with fire; "Just swim!!' she forces eye contact. She knows it's not in my interests to get out so has buried her immediate inclination to go into first-aid-mode. "It's not far - do you hear me? It's not far! You can do it - just keep going and you'll get there!" I take some deep breaths, hang back off the boat and try and relax. No chance - I'm wired tighter than something really tight and everything hurts. There's nothing I can say so I just hang there and scream in frustration for a few seconds figuring that might do the trick.

And that's the pattern for the next hour or so while I get slower and slower and the stops get longer and more frequent. It takes me 4.5 hours but eventually I do get there. It's a beautiful spot and the weather is glorious and all of us who started, successfully completed - but I just plain don't care. I'm mentally stuffed and just sit on the beach and stare at nothing for a while with a face like thunder wondering what I have to do to nail this thing.

6
Resurrection!

Monday, 7th - Wednesday, 9th July

So why yesterday? My diary sums it all up really: 'STRESS + FEEDS = SHIT.'

I had a crap week, really crap, and as late as Thursday I was not going to do that swim... but I persuaded myself that I should. I already have a stress pattern very nicely established (thank you) which has manifested itself as problems in most of the big swims. Against that background the result was almost inevitable.

There is also clearly a problem with my feeds and I suspect the culprit is the gels.

Once again, my diary for July 6 records the changes I need to make:

- *Change the feeds*
- *Visualise*
- *Rehearse*
- *Affirm*
- *Body Check*

It's the evening of July 8 and Charly is reclining post-run in her usual bath to be interrupted by Mr Happy who drags himself in and props himself up against the toilet.

While she's been out working I've done bugger all at home this afternoon, just mooching around finding things to do to distract me from having to do any work remotely associated with Arch to Arc. I'm feeling small and pissed off with myself and start to mumble on about Sunday. She eyes me steadily, "Are you feeling a bit intimidated?'

Ouch. That one hit the spot. There's a long pause while I summon the courage to admit what I've been feeling for a while now: "'Yeah... I guess I am a bit..."

"Well, that's OK isn't it? Isn't that what you teach with your clients?"

"Well... yes..." And this, of course, is part of the problem. I'm Super Coach: A Man Who Can Do Anything At All - Even Huge and

Big And Scary! I know all the theory and I even know a lot of the practical. Hey - I do this shit for a living, right? This is just another dimension but the principles are the same, right? And I have to walk this because if I don't I'm just all talk and that makes me a fraud, right - 'cos it says so in my own press releases!

More fundamentally than this though is that I've forgotten why we're doing this, yeah, that's right, WE. Charlotte and I. The Team. Us. For Better or Worse, and all that.

Charly warms to her theme "So take Sunday: it was BEAUTIFUL. The coastline was gorgeous, and you saw it from an angle very few people do - and you're unlikely to do it again. Did you take time to appreciate it?"

Well, I did a bit...

"It doesn't matter if you don't do this thing in the end. It really doesn't. But people have to see you being positive, especially in Portland, with those people who are supporting you, and Sunday... well, it was just obvious that you weren't."

We finished off some 2 hours later down the pub. That's right - us. Down the pub. Tuesday night. Well, if you're going to break a pattern then you may as well make sure..!

And the secret to this thing?

- *Relax and body check in the water*
- *Think and remember silly things to pass the time: lyrics, poems, phrases, jokes, lists.*
- *If I gotta go - just go!*
- *I KNOW I can do this. I've done everything (swim) asked of me so far - just keep progressing*
- *Pressure is simply a reflection of my ambition SO I WELCOME IT!*
- *Remember why we're doing this*
- *Smile, smile, smile and remember she loves me!*
- *Oh yeah, and change the feeds...*

And for some strange reason I slept really well that night.

Thursday, 10th July - Big Swim Day

6am: Run round Portland Bill 50 mins or so in the sea mist trying not to fall down a cliff!

2pm: Completed 6 hours 15 minutes swim.

Sorted. Nailed. Put away. Delivered. A Breakthrough... and SOOOOOO welcome! Another lovely day and could've done more. The first time I've felt 'in the groove' - time just passing and me just swimming. We even caught some fish!

Eddie: "You looked better at 5 hours that you did at 4. I was really worried after Lulworth: your face just said 'FAILURE' after the race. If you had not've delivered today I would've said No, that's it, it's all over. Well done, buddy!"

And a big weekend training followed.

7
Going For The '8'

Thursday, 17th July - Big Swim Day

The alarm sounds at 5.30am for an 8am start. My good weather spell has been broken. It's dry but blowing hard. Charly and I have spoken about this during the week and, in the safety and comfort of our living room, the prospect of some stormy weather seems fine - an interesting change even! I'm calm and looking forward to it. The target is 8 hours.

We're doing the ole canoe-to-boat routine again to get an early start. I know 8 hours was do-able, just, last week, but that was in ideal weather which today is definitely not.

Our plan to head SE through Portland Harbour is quickly scuppered. It's just a wee bit too rough for Ed in the canoe and I'm having a fun ole time as well. So we backtrack and head for the protection of the lee of the land. No worries, just relax and swim with the conditions. Don't get phased by the odd mouthful of water, waves breaking over me, or the fact that various parts of my body are periodically hanging out of the water in thin air. Just accept what Mother Nature chooses to bestow this day.

I'm quickly into my stroke this time which is pleasing as I've not swum for 3 days. Slightly unusual, but I've changed tack slightly as I gear up to these big swims. The goal is to complete them - and they're interesting enough without going into them with tired shoulders.

Through a calm section in the lee of the land, then it's back into the rollercoaster as we cut back across the harbour. I'm delighted to see Eddie wrestling with his canoe. It's entertaining viewing and helps me relax. It's still a lesson in being humble in the face of Neptune and, to get through it, I need to employ what is commonly known as a 'flexible response', roll the body more, arms higher over the top of the water, turn the head and look behind to breathe and be prepared to hold a breath if I'm about to take a mouthful of wave, Oh yeah, and swim normally when I get the chance!?!

We clear the harbour arms but Mr Ocean is still frisky. Hey - I need to be able to do this shit! (Last time I was in water this rough was the 1986 Canterbury Triathlon. Thank god for muscle-memory!) Relax, relax, relax, roll, clear the water, breathe when and where you can, smooth, smooth, trust the laws of physics - you're getting there!

Rendezvous Tom, and I get a huge thumbs-up from the man at the wheel which makes me smile around a mouthful of water. Much to Eddie's relief we're into the support boat phase heading into Weymouth Pier. Now I know Ed and Tom have to stop off to meet Wendy and a TV crew who are filming her final preparation for her Channel crossing, and I did offer to swim around in circles as background interest... but I'm not exactly clear how this will work... and I'm neither exactly full of beans or warm and toasty at this stage after nearly 4 hours in this watery rollercoaster.

Here it comes: 'Andy, just swim circles round here for a bit will you?' Tom and Ed draw imaginary loops around the shelter of the pier. Now I know that stopping and starting is death and movement is good. It's also a rare chance to catch some still water. Much to the bemusement of spectators on the pier who have seen me swim over from Portland, I proceed to cruise around clockwork-mouse-style, catching periodic glimpses of the speedboat-bound camera crew zipping around Wendy. I also know that this will take longer than Tom or Ed think, so just be cool, relax, keep swimming... it's all about the duration.

After about half an hour the commercial break is over, normal service resumes and I'm back at the boat for a feed. I've taken stock in the meantime. "I want to do 6," I announce. "It's rough, I'm not comfortable, (my stomach and bowels are participating again today though not as actively as previously) and I'll be really happy to do what I did last week in worse conditions." Eddie never hesitates, "That's fine, you're doing really well and all this messing about hasn't helped. We'll take you out to the harbour wall and you can get out when you want - no worries." He can see that this is not a time to argue. Interestingly, these are the first words of encouragement he's said all morning, and while I'm used to this 'just get on and do it' attitude, today this makes a big difference. I'm happy we have a consensus and my efforts are recognised. I know I am doing well in a big-ass sea - but it's nice to hear it from outside my own head.

Back out into the rough stuff...

After a 6 hour effort I'm back in the boat, shivering doing the coffee-shaking routine, as we chug into harbour. I'm sore, tired and very pleased. It's yet another progression on a week ago and the mood in the boat among the 3 of us is good. Would we do the crossing in those seas? "Not a chance" says Eddie. "it would be too much in the Channel - you just wouldn't get a respite." '

"You've done well today, And" notes Tom - and I know praise doesn't come lightly here! "You coped with that pretty good. It'll give you the confidence to go through the rough stuff in the Channel. All you've got to do is keep building up your hours. Push for an 8 next time if the weather's good, then just make sure you get your 10 in before the end of August." I catch Ed's eye as I know he wants me to push on earlier. The sooner I get the big stuff in, the more time for recovery I have. "Most people can cope with a third more pretty well" continues Tom. "If you've done a 6 you can cope with a 9, and if you've done a 9 you can cope with a 12."

It's only 8 weeks since I was struggling to do 2 hours, and now 8 hours is very definitely on. We're still progressing.

The day finishes with an easy run with Ed around the cliffs of Portland being entertained with stories from Mr Ette's eclectic childhood. Now let me at those calories!

8
The Boundaries Start To Move

Friday, 18th - Sunday, 20th July

Staying in the area for a few days as a bunch of old college friends are getting together for a weekend under canvas at Corfe Castle. This is usually an opportunity for me to do my sheepdog impression by accompanying the group mountain bike ride on foot while catching up with news from some top folks I've not seen for a while. So a pleasant few days pass exploring the local area on two wheels or two legs while the weather continues to bless us.

Monday, 21st - Sunday, 27th July

Another bodily change, apart from the general metamorphosis from biking legs to swimming shoulders, is that I now get stiff if I have a day of no training and no massage. Such are the training volumes I presume. This is particularly noticeable this week as I spend more time on the sponsorship / profile tasks for the Attempt. Charly has taught herself website design so that we can re-vamp mine and add all the Arch to Arc news and diaries to it. It looks great and we're getting some great feedback, but it is a product of hard and continual work.

On Monday I hear from the Royal Life Saving Society who want to meet to see if we can link up. It's the first big sponsorship break and I can see lots of potential links - but will they be able to? We meet later in the week and the vibes are good: 'So why would you want to support the RLSS?' I'm asked. 'Well, my first job was as a lifeguard...' Kinda clinches it I hope.

More and more people are starting to hear about news of the Attempt and we're both being passed good wishes by folks we know well and some we don't!

There's some real good stuff - like this particular email:

' Just read week 7/8 diary.
Keep going you crazy fool!
You're the only person who can do this.

I don't know anyone else who would even try.
That makes you special.
You could always install a Velcro fastening on the crutch of the
wetsuit?'

Chicken soup for the soul, anyone?

It's a good week: I'm sleeping like a dead thing and training pretty well. Mum comes down to stay for a few days, and while this is definitely good news for the garden (!) it also gives us a chance to do the mum-and-son bit, which doesn't happen all that often. Quite naturally, she is concerned for Number 1 Son's safety (my sanity is beyond redemption) and while much of the content of my diaries are not exactly geared towards happy-smiley - she is clearly also a little excited about the whole thing!

We end the week in the Lake District in glorious weather, though our plans to swim in Windermere are definitely thwarted by copious amounts of tupperware. Death by jet-ski is not something I particularly want to encourage!

Cold water training in the Lake District

Thursday, 31st August - Big Swim Day

No drama, no excitement, just cool resolution. Today is 8 hours. I've been quiet all week and am wearing my 'Game Face', periodically focus in, filter out, gear up, get ready and believe. Fortunately not much working with clients this week, I'd have frightened the life out of 'em!

Driving down last night Charly and I shared some thoughts on the phone. "I feel good" I'd said, "I just want to put this thing away now." And the big change of course, is that now I really believe...

The usual breakfast routine in the Ette household is a buoyant affair as the main characters put on a spirited display of martial banter to their specially invited audience! It sets the day up and only slightly distracts me from calculating and preparing what I will need for 14 feeds or so. No mean feat itself!

It's cloudy and warm with a slight breeze. Maybe rain later but I'm sure I won't notice. We're in Weymouth Bay parallel to the shore. Ed will walk the beach for the first 2 hours then Tom will pick him up in the boat. I get changed on the promenade - hey, I'm just off to work like the rest of you! - and quickly into the water. I don't even stretch but slip quickly and easily into my stroke and head east along the bay. Short strokes to start with then smooth, smooth, relax, body check and light kicks periodically to help keep it all loose! I register something doesn't feel quite right and work out that I'm not wearing my nose clip - how did that happen? - so head for the beach and retrieve it from a bemused Eddie.

And the first couple of hours just pass. It's coming easily. I'm just focused on staying relaxed and smooth and keeping the stroke turning over. I periodically glimpse Ed chatting to the locals so figure he's not too bored. The way I've figured it is simple. Stay easy for 2 hours which gives me to 6 to go - and I know I can do 6, so there's the 8.

Heading back towards Weymouth Pier the by now familiar shape of Tom's boat comes into view. After a while the dolphin-like shape I am clearly producing(!?) is spotted and the boat turns to parallel me. I get the ole double thumbs-up and return the salute with my left hand as it clears the water, and throw in a cheesy grin for good measure as I breathe to the left. Normal service has resumed.

I spot Wendy in the back of the boat. She was due to swim the Channel last week but spent 5 frustrating days in Dover waiting for the weather to clear - which it never did long enough to give her the window she needed. She will try again over the next 2 weeks, but it has brought home the importance of the weather window for my own attempt. I know there is a very real possibility that I get to Dover and I am delayed or even stopped by bad weather and there will be nothing I can do about it. She will join me for her own 3 hours today and I am looking forward to the company.

We clear Weymouth and head for the Portland Harbour arms. I spot my biggest jellyfish yet - a good dustbin lid size - as we plough through the rougher water. Wendy drops in at the next feed and heads off. I struggle to spot her in the waves but make an effort to close up. I know I should be able to match her fairly easily but after a while I'm aware that I'm working harder than I really ought to be - and Wendy is still with me. Am I struggling or is Wendy swimming faster than usual? If she is I should be able to keep with her - shouldn't I? Still, any faster and it will tip my own effort too much in the wrong direction, so I force my competitive juices down and go back to what I should be doing, focusing on me! (I find out later that Wendy was swimming to instructions, "go out hard for the first half" and that Ed was impressed because from what he could see I wasn't interested in getting into a race with her!?! Ah, if only he knew!)

We hit the rough stuff as we cross the North Ship Channel, "Stay close in!" shouts Tom, as the last thing he needs is to get his charges mown down by boat traffic. I completely get my line wrong and grovel about for what seems like ages as the sea throws me around like the insignificant rubber-clad idiot I am. Wendy has got it right though, and has put 150 yards on me. I close up in the sheltered water but guess what, the same thing happens as we cross the East Channel as well!

The loud blast of a ships horn makes me look up sharply. A navy frigate is nosing out of the harbour and very definitely filling my vision! Now these things are big, but look even bigger from water level, and even though it must be at least a quarter of a mile away it looks right on top of us! Grinning with delight at the break in the monotony - yes, really! - I realise I'd better get my shit together and swim or be re-classified 'collateral damage'!

Three hours and things are starting to get interesting. I'm very definitely tightening up in the shoulders and the hips and am slowing down. Was it the big pool session yesterday or upping the ante with Wendy? I focus hard on staying relaxed and smooth and make a beeline for the sheltered water. At the next feed my spirits are still high but now it's quite painful and the doubts are starting to creep in. Tom is adamant that I get some painkillers down me. I'm non-committal and swim off in relax-smooth focus.

It's no better next feed and Tom hands me the magic potion. I'm not strong enough to refuse it and so get it down my neck like a good 'un. The feeds are coming faster now. I'm just doing the mechanics and starting to lose track of time. For some bizarre reason I've had 'Onward Christian Soldiers' in my head for the last hour or so, and it's obviously striking a chord even if I can't get past the first few lines!

I've not been aware of Wendy for a while now then I spot her in the boat which means 3 hours have passed - but did she get in on my 2 or 3 hour mark? As we cruise into Weymouth to drop Wendy off I'm still unsure whether I've finished or not. Is this really 8 hours? It can't be, can it? Dead right: "2 hours to go!" shouts Ed as Wendy prepares to leave. Tom hands me a feed. "Up the rate, And. Just swim around her for a bit while we get sorted and we'll head across the bay - but you need to up it." Eddie hands me my 'reward' food, Jaffa cake. 'Full moon - half moon!' I grin after taking a bite. Nothing much wrong here then.

And I've been feeling better for the last half hour or so. 2 hours. OK, lets just get to 7 and take it from there. "We'll feed you every half hour!" shouts Eddie. I'm already gone.

Now it's definitely rough even with a slight following current. I know it'll be fun on the way back, but I also know I swim well into the tide. Stay smooth...

Feed 2 and we turn, let's just put this thing away! I kick and attack what I know will be the last leg. Ed has a bet with Tom that I'll do the return leg faster and for a time it looks as though I might. I feel good and am grinning insanely as I plough into the waves, c'mon you *!$*er - is this all you can throw at me?!?

Bang! Something hits my left arm and I look up to find the keel of the boat almost between my shoulder blades. What the ****!!!! I pull and kick hard to get away and stop and look back at the boat. It's the third time this has happened today. I have learned that Tom will zig-zag every now and again which is one reason why I usually keep my distance from the boat. I've been cool the previous two times and have just got on with my swim, but after over 7 hours in the water even my legendary tolerance is slipping. Still, I bite down on the worst of the expletives which are competing for space in my brain. 'Look - just give me a ****ing point to swim to and I'll swim there! Where are we going - where?!?! "Parallel the shore" comes the reply. I think **** it! fix on the Pavilion and get my head down and take my fury out on the waves...

...which is of course foolish as inevitably I run out of steam and the sea doesn't! I ease back and just cruise. My good humour has returned quickly as I start to let the achievement sink in, though I also register that I'm sore just about everywhere as well.

Just another 8 hour day at the office!

Reflections

"Hello, Swimming Husband."

"Hello, Beautiful Wife." A kiss, big hug and huge smile greet me as I step through the door early the following morning in order to catch Charly before she goes to work. Over a cup of tea we swap news and chatter and just share Something Quite Big, the first of the two key markers and suddenly everything seems so much closer. Our eyes say it all and we both find it ironic that an 8 hour swim - in itself a huge achievement - is just a step towards Something Bigger. While we are both excited, it is because we now know that this thing is definitely on...

I want to ask her to be on the support boat during the crossing. We've previously shied away from this - not least because in Eddie's experience 'partners' are not helpful when in close proximity during a Channel swim. My earlier experiences have also reinforced this: I simply did not want her (and she agreed) to experience the trauma of what I believed the crossing would be about. Much of the training has just been raw, and she saw much of this during the Lulworth swim.

Eddie, Lynne and I talked about this on Wednesday night. "Thought any more about who you want on the boat?" asked The Man Who Has.

"Well, I'm thinking more and more about asking Charly..." I reply. Ed nods over his beer. "Normally I'd say no - but she's switched on. She was on the ball when we both walked the beach for you that time at Chesil, and from what I saw she did good at Lulworth. You've got to be really comfortable with whoever it is - but I'd have no problem with her, I think she'd be a good choice." And that pretty much settled it. Ed has to be comfortable with whoever it is - there's no room to hide on that boat...

For me, of course, it is much more than this. This whole project is changing us, bringing us closer as a couple, and the swim will be the crux. How can I not share this with her - especially now that I absolutely positively believe that I can put this thing away? We will talk tonight...

Funny how your boundaries shift... An hour later I'm down the local pool getting ready for an easy paddle chatting to two swimming friends who have just finished their usual morning session. Keith & Andy are part of a small group of us who train together regularly at Hinckley. "So how did it go?" asks Keith. "Well, between 3 and 5 and a half hours were tough - and the last hour and a half were in some pretty rough stuff..." There's a short silence while they both look at each other, and I realise what I've just said: I'm talking casually about parts of what for most people is a normal day at work - but I've just been swimming it! "Bloody hell." Andy says it for them both - and these guys are good athletes but 90 minutes in the pool is considered a big session - "I was shivering at the prospect of 2 laps around Bosworth Lake without a wetsuit on Tuesday!"

Funny how fast the boundaries shift once you've got 'em moving...

On looking forward...

There's a section in one of the biographies about Daley Thompson, (Daley Thompson: The Subject is Winning) where he talks about anticipating his first Olympic Decathlon nearly one year away. It goes something like this:

'Winning in Moscow is the most important thing in my life. I think about it all the time. I'm impatient. I want to get there and do it. It's like looking forward to a good movie. You can't wait till you go, especially if it's a good show. And this is going to be a good show. July 25 and 26th. I fantasize about those days and how well I'll do. The day after doesn't mean anything to me. I'm not into that yet. I'm only up to the last day...'

It's a piece I've started to remember as I go through the same thing. It's been every day for at least the past week that I'm now starting to live the attempt in technicolour and surround-sound. In my mind the image and sounds and experiences are so real that the hairs on the back of my neck stand up. It's taken more than 2 months to get here, but NOW I'm positively salivating at the prospect!

Saturday, 2nd August

We are in Doncaster for a family wedding. I've trained early in the morning and we are carrying emergency food supplies to keep me sane through the formal proceedings. Late in the evening Mum digs out one of my junior school reports she has found during a recent tidy out: 'Andrew likes a challenge...' is the observation recorded sometime in the mid 1970's...

Sunday, 3rd August

One of those special days. The weather is gorgeous and Charly and I are at one of our favourite haunts in Clumber Park north Nottinghamshire. I'm running and Charly is on her mountain bike and we are exploring the forest trails, and like most popular visitor destinations, once you leave the immediate vicinity the crowds vanish: it's just us and the forest. My legs are heavy and it's a slow start, but then the magic begins and we just go faster and faster and faster - for 2 hours. Flashing over the trails at what feels like close to 5 minute miles I am completely and utterly in control. We both grin manically at each other... just how fast could this thing go?!

9
Ups And Downs

Monday, 4th - Tuesday, 5th August

Two days of no training and working long and late on Arch stuff, (sponsorship, profile and diaries!) and our finances. Business money worries rear their head again along with that nightmare for us self-employed: late payers. So by Tuesday night I'm a basket case and have gone into my cave... which is nice!

Wednesday, 6th August

Who is David Shephard? Well, this is what the website has to say: *'Chairman and Head of Research & Training for The Performance Partnership. More than a decade ago David left his career in electronics and IT to begin his quest to discover how to enable people to create the life of their dreams. His ferocious curiosity led him to study personal development at many levels, from the purely scientific to the truly magical. He has the ability to take the most complex ideas and distill them into a simple system that any one can learn and use.'*

Interesting enough for me to battle through traffic to be in London on a sweltering day to meet him, and interesting enough for him as a chance to conduct a series of perhaps unique field experiments with some of his techniques!

I have been introduced through one of my coaching friends who has trained under him in neuro-linguistic programming techniques. I know from my own research that David is one of the top bods at this - and I use simple variations of many of these themes in my own stuff - so I know this shit works!

What is intriguing is the opportunity to work with one of the world leaders to test some of these 'brain-programming' techniques during a huge physical challenge such as mine. I already know that this whole thing is as much mental as physical, so when the idea was first mooted around the time I was struggling to break through to 6 hours in the water I was really enthusiastic. Now though, with a successful 8 hours under my belt, I am not so sure I want to mess with what is clearly very close to being a winning formula! Yesterday, when I was doing 'crap' particularly well, I was simply resenting it as a waste of potentially good training time - which of course is just bloody ridiculous, as my dear wife pointedly mentioned on a few occasions! The actual and potential benefits of this meeting are just HUGE.

So I'm in London, and of course the meeting goes well. We look each other in the eye, share a few fundamentals, and agree some techniques which will complement what I am doing already, and arrange a session at the end of the month to work on these. I'm MUCH happier when I leave as this is clearly a great opportunity for us both.

Thursday, 7th - Saturday, 9th August

I start to feel decidedly jaded. It is still bloody hot everywhere. The UK's highest temperature records are seriously under threat and looking back over my diary I notice the last 4 weeks have been around 20 hours training a week, on top of everything else. Perhaps it's no wonder I'm a little jaded.

I rally on Friday and do a 'Mini Arch to Arc' which amounts to nearly 7 hours of run-swim-cycle in 30 degree plus temperatures. This goes really well, but I am very sore the following day - cumulative from the heat yesterday as much as the effort itself - and sleep the whole way down to Portland in the car. Shuffling is the preferred form of locomotion for the rest of the day... Oh to be a highly tuned athlete!

Sunday, 10th August - Special Swim Day
The 8 mile Round Portland Swim

It's a glorious, glorious day. Eddie wonders how I do it. I have had only one bad weather day throughout the whole swim training. A change of routine today includes Charly with Ed in the support boat skippered by Ron The Free-Diver. I will swim clockwise round Portland, a trip of some 8 miles during which I will encounter different water conditions. This swim has only been done once before by Ed's wife Lynne during her own Channel preparations last year - but I'm the first bloke, (and the first wuss to do it in a wetsuit!) Ron and Ed have decided in the week that the tides will be running right for the swim - otherwise I risk getting swept out to sea around Portland Bill! Ron briefs me as we motor about at the harbour entrance over the wreck of HMS Hood - sunk to deny the harbour to the Germans during the last war. "An hour and a quarter to the Portland Bill lighthouse," he says. I do the maths and work out that's a bloody fast first half or so, but Ron has explained that I will pick up the tide after the first checkpoint about 2 miles away. After that it's stay close around the lighthouse on the headland then work into the current all the way back to Chesil Beach. There's the unmistakable sound of a gauntlet hitting the deck and Eddie is grinning broadly: "Two and a half hours - just over, I reckon!" Are you kidding?!? I did Lulworth in over 4 and that was 10 miles! It's just the beer talking and I can't really get my head around the speed anyway, so figure I just better get going and find out...

With Eddie and Ron - somewhere above HMS Hood

Ron's right, the first feed's come and gone and I am now flying along towards the Bill. Although the stroke rate is at it's usual mid 60's I'm also working the stroke hard as the rush of the swim gets hold of me. This is just brilliant! I'm grinning from ear to ear as I gain steadily on the lighthouse ahead.

My favourite swim shot. Rounding Portland Bill Lighthouse on the Round Portland Swim.

Then it's all change as I reach the headland where the currents meet and it's very different swimming. Ron points me urgently shorewards where I am less likely to get swept out and more likely to get round. Stay relaxed, stay smooth, but work and get in close. We eventually round the point so it's safe to stop and feed, and hey presto - it's about 80 minutes! It's great to see the spectacular headland from the sea and I pause for longer than normal to take it all in. The familiar figure waving from the cliffs is Lynne who is following our swim AND briefing passing tourists on the idiot out there in the water AND checking that her instructions to my trusty crew to delay me by fair means or foul so I don't better her swim time are being carried out?!?

Now it's all about working the trip towards Chesil, and while the support boat heads closer to the cliffs to look for puffins, I enjoy the solitude of the sea - but also get mobbed by sea birds who apparently mistake me for a dolphin feeding on the surface! 'Gotta be the smooth swimming style...

While I keep the rate constant and the effort under control I get increasingly aware that I am hauling a tired body through the waves and I have to concentrate more and more to maintain my form and progress against the current. But it's just a beautiful day and fabulous scenery and my swimming has improved heaps, so despite a dubious attempt by the crew to delay me with a completely unnecessary late feed, (!) Chesil Beach arrives after around 2 hours 50 minutes of just what the doctor ordered.

Monday, 11th - Friday, 15th August

Backed right off the training for a couple of days and kept it short and sharper. Signs are that I am starting to look over the edge of the abyss - and as the consistency bit has been going really well, I sure as heck don't want to blow it now.

More naps are definitely part of the remedy...

An opportunity therefore to really nail the sponsorship part - and a couple of very long days did just that. I've not wasted time on 'cold calls' but concentrated on folks who know me and/ or whom I have worked with over the last two and a half years. By the end of Tuesday I complete putting contacts out to all those I'd planned to.

It's all a bit nervy though: while Charlotte and I have decided we can find the funds if we have to, it would make SUCH a difference to even cover half the costs of the attempt. To make matters even more interesting, all is not rosy at Charlotte's place of work, so we spend a couple of days soul searching and planning in the context of these little gems:

- *'Not getting the results you want? Change your approach!'*
- *' Focus on the things YOU can influence!'*
- *'The tough stuff is easier if you share it (with the right people!)'*

We still had a few wobbly moments though…

On Wednesday I finished reading Ellen MacArthur's book: now how small do I feel?!?

Later that day I put away a 4 hour run again in hot weather. I feel worse than expected and while some of this is dehydration I feel much is also cumulative fatigue. It's the final indicator I need, so I resolve to back right off till Big Swim Day on Saturday and spend Thursday catching up on sleep and diary work before travelling to Portland early Friday.

Saturday, 16th August

Today is Big Swim Day. I'm up at 3am listening to the wind and rain from the comfort of Eddie and Lynne's guest room. By 5am I've half convinced myself we won't swim - but get up and breakfast anyway as we have planned to be in the water for 8am. By 6am I've definitely decided we won't be, and have also now re-planned the rest of the weekend and am positively salivating at the prospect of added recharge time! Eddie walks in "We've been out in worst than this, buddy - let's go out as planned!" Bollocks. In my mind I am already up the M5… Eddie looks over giving me that marine corps 'just how big are they' look. "It 'd be easy to bin it - we need to swim!" Oh shit. Shit, shit, shit, shit! I've been building a really good case since 3am and now I have something any prosecution would struggle to pick holes in. I'm tired physically and mentally and I know I don't HAVE to do this today - we still have 5 weeks to go. Just let me re-charge a bit and I'll come back and nail this on Thursday!

I try a few lame excuses but I also don't want to let these guys down. Ed and Lynne were up late last night and here they are early this morning because they've committed to helping some idiot do this London to Paris thing… And I know I can do this if I had to so… "OK" I reply trying to sound convincing, "Let's swim!"

My head re-programming is however, not needed. Eddie steps out of the car on Portland Harbour an hour later, takes one look at the surf and pronounces, "No way! It's much worse than I thought it would be - you just wouldn't get a respite in this and it'd kill you!" I grin weakly trying to do my best 'aw shucks' expression, but The Man Who Has hasn't finished and flashes an evil grin in my direction. "We could walk the shore with you so you could get thrown around for a couple of hours though if you want - good practice!" Fortunately at this point I remember that I've already done 'thrown around' for around 6 hours some weeks ago, so calculate that it's pretty safe to respectfully decline...

Funny how it all turns out though... we were only remarking a few days ago that we have been able to do all the planned swims - something that Eddie has never done with any of his Channel folks - and that the law of averages says we will get a spanner in the works at some point.

Just this small matter of 10 hours remains... till next week!

10
The Final Big Test

"I wish I could help you more with the sponsorship stuff," says Charlotte on Tuesday morning after I pick up two 'no thanks' emails from my two Big Sponsorship Hopes. We've taken stock again last night and chewed it through some more with friends Malcolm and Rhona who came over for dinner. I know that the best thing I can do is to get myself physically and mentally as ready as I can be for this thing - and capitalise on it all afterwards. Anything we are able to do before the Attempt is a bonus - but it really is getting a little unnerving when put against my business situation and Charlotte's current work environment. Still, this is why we do these things and we're actually not machines. OK if I do bottom lip wobbling every now and then, please?

Friday, 22nd August - Very Big Swim Day!
"'You've lost count now, haven't you?" Eddie is grinning round a mug of tea. It's 6am in the Ette household and I'm performing complex mathematical equations against the usual backdrop of good natured banter: now how many feeds do I need and was that the 5th or 6th scoop of powder..?
Somehow the conversation has got round to the delicate balance between performance in the bedroom and in the field of athletic endeavour - particularly when in heavy training. I've just remarked that of the times Charly and I are together at the moment, I seem to spend most of 'em asleep! "Ah, it worked the other way for me," Ed counters with a twinkle in his eye, "I was definitely more, er, active!" Lynne rolls her eyes while I contemplate the innate unfairness of the situation - then console myself my rationalising that I clearly must be training far harder than Eddie did!?!
Back to the business at hand...

A 10 hour swim means:

- 12-14 feeds plus some for emergencies. 4-5 scoops of carbohydrate powder per 2 feeds, 2-4 feeds per bottle depending on size all made with boiling water: 5 hot bottles plus one of cold water.
- 1 x personalised 1/4 litre wide mouth feed bottle on a string to decant into.
- 1 x malt loaf cut into chunks.
- 2 x bananas.

That's the staple stuff. For rewards and treats:

- Jaffa cakes and jelly babies (assorted) plus tea - usually from Tom.
- For emergencies: carbohydrate gels x 3 and energy bars x 2.
- For variety: 1 x can fruit cocktail chunks.

Post swim: macaroni cheese on toast, bread and butter pudding (homemade) and tea. Loud, raucous music for the drive home!

Feed Stop

Today I have an appointment with the sea for 10 hours and I want to get it done. This is almost the final piece of the preparatory jigsaw: completion will mean we really are 'good to go'.

While I am not nervous there is some trepidation - though I have no doubts I will do this. The only thing that will stop me is bad weather, and even then I am prepared to go out and do battle for as long as I can! I've also deliberately put in about 15 hours training already this week- so I'm going into this less than fresh - but I've eaten well and grabbed plenty of naps so I figure I'm as ready as I'll ever be.

My thoughts turn frequently to Charlotte as this will be a pretty tough day for her: even when she finishes work for the day I will still be in the water. I remember that she has a busy morning and figure that this will help her.

Lynne gives me a bigger hug than normal as we prepare to leave: she's been here herself and knows what's at stake. Wendy has also sent her good wishes, so there's a few people rooting for me today...

I'd hoped we'd simply head east down the coast from Weymouth to Lulworth and back - a trip of some 20 miles - but this is so weather dependent. While it is fine and warm it is blowing Force 3-4 from the SW which mean that in the battle of sea and swimmer, the swimmer loses! We will therefore be dog-legging around the bay which is mentally tougher - but then it's gonna be that kind of day...

So just after 8am we clear Weymouth Harbour and I take a header off the side of the boat to get this show on the road. I'm following the line of the 8 knott buoys straight across the bay and then we'll simply turn and re-trace to collect Tom from the pier so he can join Ed for the rest of the day.

Despite a stroke rate which is lower than normal (60: I'm really doing 'relaxed' this morning!) the following wind and current mean I fly down the bay and make the turn in well under the hour. The return trip is certainly more interesting as I'm swimming straight into wind, waves and current - though at this stage it's all just adding spice!

Half past 10 and we're back at the harbour to collect Tom and I get the pep-talk, "We'll take it back across the bay again then down the coast as you did for Lulworth. Just do like Wendy and Lynne did - nice and steady all the way through and you'll be fine." The boys are already trailing the fishing lines, they've got enough food to survive a siege and the sun is coming out. I figure they'll be OK.

Once again I'm tide-assisted back across the bay - haven't I been here before somewhere? - then turn SE to follow the coast. Now it really is getting interesting: I'm broadside onto the wind and swell and the sea is now blowing Force 4. Stay smooth, don't fight it, you've been in bigger stuff than this. The boat's having a worse time than me - side on means it is getting thrown about big-time...

Just after midday - I'm using the position of the sun to measure time passing - and Feed 5 comes around. My stroke rate has dropped to the mid-50's in this rough stuff, but all is still in the green, though a vaguely unsettling thought has begun to surface: if I've got this sea to contend with all the way to Lulworth AND I simply get battered from the other side when we turn and come back, it sure will make for an interesting day at the office! Oh well, one thing at a time...

An hour later Ed is standing in the boat and indicating a change of direction. I swim over for confirmation "Head straight for Portland!" "Straight across?" I query. "All the way," comes the reply "just head straight into the waves!" They've obviously got fed up being tossed about broadside on - it's far better facing directly into the elements. More importantly, I could be in trouble later on if we continue as there is no shelter here and I will just eventually run out of steam from continually battling this sea. I don't know it at the time, but I'm facing about 5-6 miles straight across the bay in a Force 4. What I do know is that I can barely see the outline of Portland ahead, I've been battered for about an hour already, and once I start this leg there will be no respite till I reach the shelter of the harbour arms on the other side.

Today is the day, so I bury my head into the oncoming wave and get on with it.

Feed 6 and I'm treated to two jelly babies as well. "Charlotte's phoned to see how you're getting on," Ed tells me. "Lynne and Wendy have also rung and Kate has sent a text message as well." He pauses. "Don't know what all the fuss is about - nobody ever phoned me when I was swimming!" I grin and then it hits me: people have taken the time and trouble to remember me on my Biggest Day and send their support. And suddenly I'm back in the Lakeland church as Charly and I exchange our wedding vows. The emotional surge is so strong I start to well up and choke down a sob which threatens to break out. Fighting down tears I push away from the boat to the privacy of the sea. The feelings of love and support are nearly overwhelming: I have to complete today - I HAVE to! I think of all we've been through to get here and that I'm still going to get my head kicked in for a few hours yet. This is SO hard, but it's a relief and a joy to be finally at this point. 'I love you, Charly!' Swimming with tears in my eyes and bottom lip periodically wobbling is definitely a whole new experience!

Looking back now I'm quite impressed I maintained forward momentum, but here's the strange thing: physically I could feel that I was OK - no aches or pains - but it would've been great just to stop, climb into the boat and have a little cry. 'It's OK,' I'd say to the boys, 'I just need to let this lot out and I'll be right back with you!'

It was a real rollercoaster in every sense for the next few feeds…

From Eddie's log:

'2pm Feed 7: Very quiet… stretched neck and kept eyes closed a lot…

2.30pm: Showed a few signs of being tired. SR 52. More mental I think. To be expected after 2 hours with face into the sea.

3pm Feed 9: Very quiet, no words spoken…'

Heading towards 4pm and the sea and I are definitely calmer. My stroke rate has picked up and I pass the 8 hour mark swimming strongly. I'm closing on Portland Harbour East entrance and it feels great to be in flatter water. I'm just cruising…

'5pm Feed 12: 'He has a smile on his face during the feed. Started to talk again - he knows!'

I sure did - after 9 hours in the water I'd only one to go, and it would be calm all the way in…

'5.40pm Feed 13: 'Happy chatty. Did not look tired. Finished at start point 6.14 pm. Charlotte phoned, Lynne phoned - all happy! Total 10 hours 4 minutes.'

Charlotte's Day (in her own words)

Andy was calm on Thursday : definitely not as removed as before the '8' - almost blasè. 'That's a good thing', I thought 'but is it too much?' Before the '8' he'd been much more in his cave - this time more relaxed...

On Friday when I got up I thought about him getting ready. I was at home till 9am. I promised myself I'd phone Eddie at half way after my meeting: I wanted to check the weather but never actually got round to it.

I had my meeting: thinking about Andy still swimming. I rang Eddie and was surprised when he answered almost immediately. I could hear the boat engine over the phone - I was right there! 'He's doing great!' Eddie told me, 'It's pretty windy but he's getting his face in like a good'un! We're coming up to a feed so I'll tell him you've rung.'

It helped that I'd lots to do that afternoon. Ian at work said Andy would come out looking like a big purple scrotum!? Some people...! I figured he'd finish about 6pm so I was able to call again from home. Eddie said they'd only got another 20 minutes to go. 'How's he doing?' I asked 'He's doing great, he's done it - only another 20 minutes!' came the reply.

I rang back and Eddie passed me over - I was surprised how coherent and together he sounded. ' Hi babe' I heard, 'I love you!' We talked briefly. I was so excited and just about to tell him how great and not shivery he sounded when , 'I need to go now and get some warm gear on!'

I was all proud and excited and spent the next few minutes skipping round the house like a looney - so much so I bumped my head on the stairway ceiling. I'm not normally that bouncey, but was just excited and had no one to tell!

And afterwards? I felt fine: a little stiff and tired to be sure, but nowhere near the sensation of having been run down by a steamroller, and better even than after the 8 hour effort. I'm very, very satisfied but I'm not going mad: in my head this is still a stepping stone - the best one yet but still only that. Tom looked over as we packed up. "The Channel's there for the taking, And - there for the taking."

The following day Charlotte and I head for the Lake District. I have a day of rest then it's out in the hills running and riding. It's glorious weather, I feel fine, and it now very definitely feels very close and very real...

Quality time with Charlotte in the Lake District

Part Two
Showtime!

"You can map out a fight plan or a life plan, but when the action starts it may not go the way you planned, and you're down to your reflexes - which means your training. That's where your roadwork shows.
If you've cheated on that in the dark of the morning - well, you're going to get found out now under the bright lights."

Joe Frazier, Boxing.

My Compelling Goal

'It's 20th September 2003. I'm World Record Holder for the Enduroman Arch to Arc Challenge. It is only the second time this has ever been done. I have lowered the existing record to 60 hours and am proud of the way I have done it. I have done it in a way which is a reflection of me and what I stand for: with humility, courtesy, honesty, integrity and appreciation of those around me.'

With help from David Shephard of The Performance Partnership: looking into the future I visualised for myself in early August.

Running

"*Pressure is just the shadow of great accomplishment... Sometimes shadows are cast longer than the thing itself, and pressure can seem like that - more weighty than the accomplishment it's reflecting. But like a shadow, there is really no substance there. move into the light and the shadows fade. Move into the shadow's way and you can block it with your own.*"

Michael Johnson, Athletics

Wednesday, 16th September

Morning - and Charly and I are at home in the garden doing a piece to camera.

"It's all less than 10 hours away now, the start has been moved forward and we're enjoying a last quiet moment. We were due to go on Thursday, but there has been much excitement in the house since this morning when we got the phone call from Portland 'We're gonna go now - get your ass to London!'

'So I'm here trying to do calm, really I'm a bit *butterflyee*, and Charly's doing very excited.

'How excited are you, Charly?"

She leans in close and her face shines "I'm very excited!"

"The phone's been going mad and that includes BBC TV: 'Hello, we're the BBC and we're interested.' 10 hours to go and NOW they're interested!?!

(Turn to face excited wife) Why am I doing all the talking, Charly?"

"Cos your so good at it, Andy! "

Fair one. Back to camera...

"So we've got a little jog at night through London. I figure it'll be quiet but they're trying to tell me something about a 24-7 capital city - probably have to run the gauntlet with kicking out time from the clubs: impromptu speed session anyone? Tomorrow we see the sea, which means it's swim-time. I plan to rest - how long? We'll see, but it'll be a start in the early hours. 12, 13, 14 - 16 hours, I don't know: I've done the training and I'm just confident I can do it Touch the French side then get back in the boat to get to Calais - how weird is that?!? Then there is just a little bike ride (180 miles) to finish with the last 30 miles into the heaving, seething metropolis of Paris. Navigation will probably be the only thing on the minds of the crew - but I can ride like a Parisian if I have to."

There're 3 key points in my mind on this jaunt:
- Finish the swim,
- Ride up the Champs Elysées
- Talk to rooms full of people about the whole thing afterwards.

And I'll take 'em all - especially the first one.

The rest of the day passes in a whirl of preparations. I had planned to sleep but it just never happens, and by 9.30pm we are en route to the start.

"We're coming into London, Andy" My wife Charlotte shakes me gently out of the short sleep I've managed to grab in the back of the motorhome and I peer out of the back window. Yep - definitely London and definitely very real! We share a nervous smile and I move to sit next to her knowing that this will probably be the last quiet moment together for the next few days. I watch the increasingly familiar sights roll past as Charly helps her brother, Tim Jury, who is driving, to find our way to Marble Arch where we are due to link up with The Two Eddies' - Clarke, our main driver, mechanic, navigator and all round top bloke, and Ette - who's World Record I'm out to take.

The final member of our crew is sitting opposite me having finished a full day in his osteopathic clinic barely 2 hours before.

I met John Williams some 3 years ago when he was lecturing on a Sports Massage course I was attending when I was getting ready to start my own business. We clicked, found out we lived and worked pretty close together and stayed in touch. For the last 2 years or so John has fixed every single one of my coaching clients I have referred him. As far as I'm concerned his professional competence is 24 carat gold, though the fact that we share the same hairstyle really clinches it. He has become a firm friend to both Charlotte and I, and I know my legs will be in great hands on the first stage.

John catches my eye "How you feeling?" I nod slowly and let a smile grow. "I'm good, I'm alright." He smiles and looks away as Charlotte squeezes my hand, not long now...

And then we're there. Tim does a circuit of Marble Arch as the rest of the guys strain to spot signs of The Two Eddies. Sure enough the unmistakable outline of a small white van is parked unashamedly centre stage. While Tim baulks only slightly at the prospect of getting 30 feet of motorhome through the Arch itself, pride dictates he manages it on the third circuit - well, we all figure we've got a great excuse to be here - and as the time edges towards midnight we roll to a stop.

Greetings and introductions are exchanged. The last time I saw Eddie Ette was some 2 weeks ago at my last training swim off Portland. The handshake is as firm as ever but the eyes say 'showtime!' He looks straight at me: "How you feeling?" I give it straight back "I'm good - so how do you want to play this, then?"

I let him make the running as I figure this part is probably more nerve-racking for him than it is for me. It's as much a first for him organising, as it is for me doing and we've both invested in the other to get at least this far. There's friendship and mutual respect in abundance and we've both seen enough of the other over the summer to know that we will both give everything we have to pull this off... we just don't know if this will be enough. I'm reminded of a phrase from my old Team Flamingo triathlon club days: 'When the flag drops, the bullshit stops.' Guess we're gonna find out, then.

Once we're away the crew will work out and settle into a routine much of which will be dictated by ME. Right now it's a little like arriving early at a party - no one wants to be the first to dance! The guys default down to their primary roles. Tim will be doing all the filming and photos and has a whole host of new toys to play with. He travelled down to us from his home in Lancashire on Monday and promptly took over our living room table as a home for cameras, bits of cameras and instruction manuals for cameras! This will very definitely be a 'learn by doing' experience, so he heads off to set up with John being co-opted for floodlight duty. Charly and Eddie Clarke review the route and make final preparations to the vehicles while Ed casts round for someone to grab as a witness signature which we need periodically to validate my progress for the Guinness Book of Records. Something along the lines of 'yes, I did see some idiot running past me at such-and-such a time at such-and-such a place trailed by a dubious looking bloke on a mountain bike, and no, it's none of your business what I was doing out so late on a weekday when most normal people are safely tucked up in bed.' For my part, I have complete faith in Ed's unique ability to co-opt anyone he cares to and relieve them of their signature as we make our way to Dover.

"Just sign here please Sir" Eddie collars our first witness

Time to get ready. I keep it slow and methodical and retreat to MY primary role. Running around like an idiot will not help me or the crew. I know the value of role models and KNOW that the guys will take a lead from me throughout this trip. If I'm cool, odds are they will be too, so I go about my final preparation without flapping.

It hits me how warm it is - heat of the city and all that - but I'm sure the temperature will drop as we head out of the city and chase the dawn. I elect to start in shorts and short sleeves. Vaseline goes onto the insides of both thighs and between both sets of toes, soles of my feet and heels and Achilles tendons. I've discovered Ron Hill single skin anklet socks over the summer and now don't use anything else: they're lightweight, breathable, quick-drying and do not ruck up. A small rub could quickly escalate and cause me serious problems. I've been careful during training to look after my feet and keep good foot hygiene - nails are kept short and smooth and calluses are filed down and smoothed off. I will change socks and re-vaseline at every stop with a shoe change at 50 miles. If it happens it happens - but I'm confident my feet will stay intact. A flouro vest and flashing red light

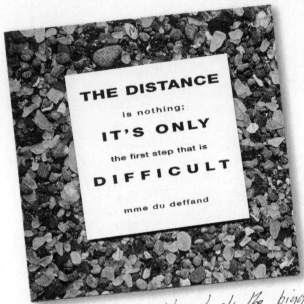

THE DISTANCE

is nothing;

IT'S ONLY

the first step that is

DIFFICULT

mme du deffand

You took the biggest step when you made the decision, now just finish the Job.

Ed

Begin at the
beginning and
go on until you come
to the end;

then stop.

Lewis Carroll Alice in Wonderland

clipped into my waistband completes the ensemble.

Outside once again and it strikes me how small Marble Arch is - I'm sure the French one is HUGE compared to this! Charly and Eddie C are talking route - the crew will split into two for this first section through London and we will rendezvous with Tim & John in the motorhome at the first stop at 20 miles. The boys are still playing with the technology so Ed and I gravitate towards each other. Conversation is about getting out of London in one piece, stay cool, relax and enjoy the sights - take it real steady and don't get freaked if we lose the route. It's big ole London Village, everyone is a tad nervous, it's all very new and everyone wants to get it right, mistakes are bound to happen. For some reason we're talking in low tones - a way to keep the tension at bay, I guess.

It's getting close. Ed hands me some cards from the Weymouth chapter of my support crew and Charly and I go in front of camera to open them. Tom, Kate, Wendy, Lynne and Ed have all sent best wishes in their own inimitable style. Kate has enclosed some photos of her own Channel swim on the most glorious of days and some of Ed getting ready for his. By the expression the camera has captured on his face, I'm relieved to see that he clearly does nerves after all!

Ed's message is all vintage Ette "You took the biggest step when you made the decision - now just finish the job."

I remember his letter of a week ago:

Dear Andy

We have spent many hours together since our first discussions about attempting the Enduroman Arch to Arc. I knew after our first meeting your character was right for the task.

You have come a long way in a very few months and in my opinion are well ready for the attempt. You know the Enduroman Team and I will be doing everything in our power to help you achieve my record. You are being guided all the way by the same Enduroman Team that helped me achieve my 2001 World Record.

As your day approaches many local people have asked me why would I spend so much of my time to help you beat my record. The reasons for this we have discussed many times. It is my opinion that your attempt will highlight the Enduroman Arch to Arc challenge to the world. It is my intention to stage this challenge for any athlete from any part of the world that has the ability to succeed...

The task you have ahead of you is massive. I know because I have been there. You are more than capable and now only require three things: True Enduroman Grit. Fine Weather and Good Luck.

Eddie Ette

Time to go: Eddie has his witnesses, the boys are ready with the toys and there's no more reasons anyone can think of to hang around. A kiss from Charly, a final check of the direction, touch the Arch with my hand and Ed starts the clock at 12.38am. The handshake is firm and the eyes say it all, let's finish this thing!

I take my first tentative steps across the courtyard and down the steps into the subway then angling up to road level trying very hard not to think of the enormity of the 87miles that lie ahead. We will pretty much follow the line of the A20 all the way to the coast but I suspect this first bit will be interesting. Ed catches me up on the mountain bike as I take in the sights and sounds of the capital city in the early hours. I'm rubber-necking big-style as I pass The Ritz. There's still plenty of people about and I would hardly say the traffic is light! I'm keeping it smooth and loping along grinning stupidly. I barely get a second glance from those I pass - clearly very little suprises the worldly wise folks down here.

The first hiccup comes after barely the first mile or so; we lose the van with Eddie C and Charly. The motorhome has gone ahead to the first stop at 20 miles but the plan has been for the van to stay as close as it can to us through the city. Easier said than done through these streets with various one-way options even at this time of night. Ed is understandably concerned but I'm cool. I can survive for 90 minutes if I have to, though I'd prefer 60! All we have to do is stay heading for the A20 and the van can backtrack for us. Just do my thing and enjoy the sights. I let Ed know I'm not flapping and hope the reassurance helps his nerves. He's already settling into a routine of racing ahead on the mountain bike to accost potential witnesses then catching back up to shout directions. I wonder how different this feels for him now...

A few miles later we have our happy re-union with the van and everyone tries hard not to be obvious about the sighs of relief. I've begun to get a little concerned as the time has ticked by and so have been busy being a tourist by way of distraction. At 1.20am I change from shirt to vest - it really is warm! - have a slurp from a carbohydrate drink and continue to pass the time talking bollocks with the boys. The first of the urban fox sightings happen and I wonder idly how many I'll eventually see.

Feed 2 comes at 1.50am with a drink and some food. I know I have to keep these brief but the final balance between movement and rest will be a delicate one. I've resolved not to put a watch on these stops but not to hang about either: get the re-charge I need then get on with it. Charly is finding her way into a routine of doze in van, wave to running bloke periodically out of the back window, and prep the feeds ready for running bloke's arrival. We have rehearsed as much as we feel we need to in the days leading up to departure, but we also know that we'll figure much of it out quickly as we go along. She's one switched-on cookie - one of the reasons I married her really... The key to this learn-by-doing in these early miles is that I must be cool, communicate clearly and preferably in advance what I want and when so the guys around me get the confidence from a working routine quickly. So keep the effort comfortable, say your pleases and thank yous and remember that everyone wants the same damn thing here! So I concentrate on giving out the positive vibes so that we all settle in as quickly as possible. Happy athlete equals happy crew - pretty simple formula really.

Four minutes later I'm on my way walking away from the feed and gradually breaking into a jog.

From Eddie's log: *2.30am Sipping carbo drink. Not drinking much. Pace remains strong. I would be drinking more.*

At 3.50am we stop for the first big feed and massage at around 20 miles - the first big marker. The pace has been very comfortable and I'm pleased with progress. This is John's first real test - so just how well can he massage while being asleep on his feet? It's pitch black, we're parked up by a roundabout on the A20 and I'm covered in my warm gear lying on the couch while John does his thing, Charly says 'hi' and does the food bit, and the rest of the boys voice their displeasure that I'm getting all the tea rations at the moment. I remember that Ed needs at least a cup each hour to function so realise that this must be a real trauma for him. Tim briefly appears from the inside of the motorhome looking like death, but the lack of tea also means that there is one more good reason not to be awake. We are now very definitely out of London, the urban fox count is at 6 and all is well with the world.

20 minutes later I'm back on my feet walking away from the crew to sounds of good-natured abuse: something about they thought I was supposed to be running this?

4.30am. Into the quiet unlit lanes now and the van is behind me with lights full beam to light the way. It's been getting steadily hillier and as I'm trying to keep the effort even I choose to walk up the steep climb of Brands Hatch Hill. We really are chasing the dawn now and I'm at the high point of the run which gives me a breath-taking vantage point of the starlit clear sky and the panorama of much of the south east below me. The fox count is up to eight and I know we will shortly be beginning the long descent into Maidstone. I wonder how my quads will find that…

From Eddie's log: *4.55am. Slight pause and walked, started to run more or less straightaway. We drove alongside and asked if OK. He looked but did not speak. First time he has not spoken. Still running well.*

5.15am and the fox count tops out at nine! I pass Ed coming out of a garage into which he has crawled to get a signature. He looks like death and I take great delight in telling him so. The reply casts aspersions on my parentage so I figure I'm the only one enjoying the graveyard shift. Daylight is almost on us and it looks like it will be a good day.

6.15am and I've stopped about a mile short of the motorhome which is parked up at the second massage stop and big feed. That last section felt longer than the planned 15 miles and I've really been looking forward to the stop for the last couple of miles or so. So I've stopped and am in 'let-the- mountain-come-to-Mohammed' mode!

From Ed's log: *6.15am. Stopped for a feed drinking carbo. Got in the back of the van and laid flat with legs raised. Talking to Charlotte. He is OK but just decided 'I have now stopped - let's get the van with the massage here!' phoned van to return.*

7am Just under 6.5 hours gone and about 35 miles covered. Started to walk on no problems. Charlotte will cycle with him for a while.

I'm on the couch while John goes to work. The boys are pissed off because Charlotte is being fiercely protective about the tea supply, I'm drinking it and they're not. It wouldn't be so bad except they've been tortured by the smell of baking bread from the local Sainsburys for the last few minutes while waiting for me to arrive. Tim comes over and does puppy-dog eyes at my mug of tea. I pretend not to notice.

"So, how you feeling - any problems?"

"Just my quads," I reply. While I've tried to control the long descent down from the high point over the last few miles, the old tell-tale signs are there. 'If there's a weakness it's my quads which go first and always the left side. Everything else is fine. I've been trying to keep it smooth, but the cumulative effect on this gig is a real killer, y'know?!'

John looks up from his ministrations "Are you on the same camber all the time?" I remember a story I heard over the summer about a Forces guy who yomped from Dover to London all on the same side of the road and gave himself hip problems for months afterwards.

"No, I'm trying to stay level - in the middle of the road where I can. I've been getting away with that through the night - different kettle of fish now though. Right through the training it's been OK, then right at the end - the last couple of weeks I started to feel it in that left side." I shrug and eye John. "Part of the reason you're here, matie!"

Ed wanders over and steals one of my Jaffa cake treats 'Full moon, half moon - total eclipse!' That advert has much to answer for... as Ed wordlessly examines some of John's kit.

It strikes me how different this must seem to Ed - it's world's apart from how he worked his own attempts. All this massage and ministrations - what are you, some kinda blouse? Just get on with it! I also know he respects that I want to do this thing how I want to do it. So we just grin at each other knowing exactly what the other is thinking.

It reminds me of the early days in Portland and the messages both verbal and non-verbal: *"You want to do this thing? Just swim! Don't think about it, don't piss about and ask questions, don't worry about where you are and how far to go. Your job is to swim - we'll tell you when to feed and when to stop. You need a couple of 6's, an 8 and a 10 hour swim and we ain't got much time - and you wont get there by fucking about. Yes, it's going to be cold, yes, it's going to be hard: it was the hardest fucking thing I've ever done. I came to hate that bloody quayside where Tom's boat was - but that's the Channel for you. You want this thing? Just get on with it!"*

Ed's just a more a Do-er while I'm more a Thinker - though I've had to work hard at combining the two especially since working for myself. An interesting collision of worlds though...

John continues his work as I remark that I'm very glad he's got his *human* bag with him as opposed to his canine one. You see, John was at our wedding in 2002 when he got into conversation with Sue my mother-in-law who was administering to her greyhound type dog at the time. In a previous life John used to race these things, so common ground was quickly established. For some reason the conversation got round to dental hygiene: 'Oh, don't worry,' pipes up John, 'I've got my bag with me, so I can sort her out now if you want.' !!!?!!? What the HECK are you doing with your dog maintenance kit at our wedding?!? Still, John got huge points as far as Sue was concerned, and became forever referred to in that part of the family as The Dog Dentist - oh, the trappings of fame!

I spot Tim still doing bleary really well. "I saw the dawn even if you didn't."

"Yeah, but I've got my long term survival at heart" comes the deadpan reply. He's still smarting over the refusal of Sainsburys to open their bakery at 5 am.

I do a piece to camera.

"7 o'clock and where are we? Just coming into Maidstone." John joins in around a particularly impressive calf stretch assist "Everyone should try this, don't you think, Andy?"

"Absolutely! It'd save the planet - and everything else..." I continue with the narrative "When we went to collect the motorhome we were the youngest, fittest and slimmest people there. The average age of the combat soldier was 50 plus, the average size was 18 - feet across. We're welcome back when we're old and fat - hey, we'll fit right in then!"

I finish with a slightly more serious bit "If I have a chink in my musculo-skeltetal armour it's my quads. Jarring is a problem - I'm OK if I keep it moving and stay smooth. We'll just manage it for this next section. The Goal is 50. If I do that I've cracked it even if I have to crawl the rest."

8am and getting through Maidstone during the morning rush has been a bitch. It'd taken me the longest yet to get running again from the stop. Walk - trot-walk-trot - run for a while till the legs get the message again. Charlotte has been with me on the mountain-bike as she has had to link with the van ahead as we weave through the town. It's a relief to get through but traffic remains very heavy - such as contrast to the quiet I've been used to so far. Still, not much I can do about it and chatting with Charly about silly things helps keep the brain busy.

We're onto long stretches of open main road heavy with traffic as we make our way to the 50 mile stop. The temperature is climbing steadily and I have a healthy sweat on. This is THE key benchmark in my mind - it's all down hill after this though it really is unknown territory. I've planned a couple of smaller 10 mile chunks to get to 70 miles but I really have no idea how I'll find it. Guess I'll be finding out pretty soon...

Baby wipes refresh the parts other wipes cannot reach! Freshening up at 50 miles

50 miles is reached in a shade over 8 hours. This is a longer than normal stop with a big massage, feed, wipe down and full kit change and plenty of talking bollocks. Everyone is smiling and chatting - pleased that we're making good progress and I'm still in good condition. The goal throughout the Challenge is to maximise the physical, mental, emotional and nutritional benefit of the stops - so I am able to look at the next section as a whole new start as

opposed to a continuation. It' s a bit like a rugby team having a wash and changing into new kit at half time. My powers of recovery have always been good as far back as I remember - all I'm doing now is taking it to another level so I am better able to look at this thing as many small steps as opposed to one 290 mile journey.

I'm back on my feet 45 minutes later and am able to break into a run after a short progressively faster walk. We've decided to break this next 10 miles at 5 miles - or about 50 minutes at my current pace - and sure enough 55 miles is reached 50 minutes later. It's a quick stop but I can tell Ed is concerned that I'm not drinking enough. The temperature is continuing to climb as 11 am approaches.

Now it's getting real interesting. I find that it is easier to break into a run while going uphill than on the flats or definitely any downhills. My legs are getting progressively stiffer and my quads are more and more solid. Knee lift is limited and I definitely wont win the style prize any more. 'Just keep moving - keep running.' I remember the line from Lance Armstrong's book as he goes through his chemotherapy. *"Get up - move! If you can still move you're OK."* I'm not looking into the distance any more - with the peak of my hat pulled right down over my eyes my vision has narrowed to the 2-3 metres in front of me. Occasionally I'll check to spot where the van is, but that function's been allocated to a distant part of the brain I'm not all that bothered about. Keep the rhythm, keep moving, keep RUNNING - just get to 60 and you'll be OK.

I force myself to break the tunnel vision every now and again by taking in my surroundings. Definitely getting rural now as we head towards Ashford. Traffic has thinned and the quality and width of the pavement tells me very few folks use it! The broken surface is not helping me but I'm buggered: running in the gutter on the road is out because I'm scared of prolonged periods on a camber, and running in the middle of the road is out because - well, it's not very sensible. And this is the routine for the next couple of miles: focus in, keep face, shoulders, arms and hands relaxed, stay smooth, keep rhythm, keep RUNNING. Look up, deep breaths, shake down, take in the sights - where's the van? - more deep breaths, then focus in...

But now I'm really starting to cook and feel tired as my mind starts to play tricks. I've been pretty good at estimating time and distance completed without using a watch - and I'm not wearing one - but as I think I'm nearing the 60 mile mark I start to pass a series of lay-bys on my left. To me, lay-bys only mean one thing: the motorhome parked up which means it's time for me to stop. So as I crest a particularly nasty short rise and the first lay-by appears, I'm looking eagerly for the motorhome. I've slowed to a walk in anticipation of the stop, (I always walk the final stretch into and out of the stops) but no motorhome. Bollocks. Oh well... but getting into a run is hard now. The van pulls up alongside from following me and Ed looks out "Just down this road, Andy - just keep it going a while longer." A while longer. Well, OK if you say so.

The second lay-by 'It's gotta be here - there's even a café - the boys will definitely have stopped by a café for 60 miles. Legs are fucked, I'm a bit bushed, but I'm here - massage and food and I'll be OK.'

But there's no van - this is not the 60 mile point. Disbelief, confusion and disappointment momentarily swamp me. The shade of the trees end, the open road starts again and no sign of the motorhome. I do stoic and get on with it - but the mental hurt is now as big as the physical.

Then there's the van parked on the verge - no motorhome: have they got lost? - but the van will do. As far as I am concerned this IS the 60 mile point. Ed gives me the good news "It's about a mile down the road - they're parked up waiting for us"

You're having a fucking laugh, I think - I'm not going anywhere. However, because I was brought up properly I make an attempt to do coherent and polite. "I just need to get out of this heat and lie down for a bit. I'm a bit bollocksed - can you get the van to come back here instead?" So while the boys get sorted I make a slow and painful attempt to lie down with legs raised in the back of the van. Closing my eyes in the shade is bliss - though I can feel my blood thumping through my body.

It's a longer than planned-for stop, but some damage has been done in that last section and I need a re-charge. Ten mile chunks are definitely far too long, and now it looks like 5 mile sections are pushing it. John has to take the longest time yet to work some range of movement and elasticity back into my legs. We have to be careful - any sudden movement will bring a yelp of pain. It's the first time I've stopped short of a planned marker and I know the crew will register what is the first real blip. I don't. In my head I'm 60 miles to the good. My quads are fucked but everything else is fine and mentally I'm great. The treat foods come out and Charly takes time to relay some goodwill messages that have come in by phone. More evidence that this is a solo challenge in name only, and I'm quickly smiling and joking.

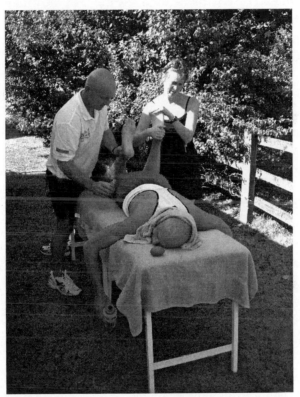

Two for the price of one; Charly & John on foot massage duty

John is starting to get concerned though, and we talk damage limitation. "Are you using your arms much?" "Not really, I'm just trying to stay relaxed and smooth." "Maybe you should bring 'em in more', he suggests, 'cos you've got to try and get your knees to lift again. Keep the knee lift and you help keep the muscle length. Everything's just tightening up at the moment and you're no better than shuffling." No kidding, I think, but I'm still fucking *running* this thing.

Half an hour later I'm back on my feet but now it's a walk-shuffle-trot-run routine which I have to repeat a few times before I can make the running bit stick. I've asked for brief stop with the van at 2.5 miles and then a longer one with the motorhome at 5 miles. A few miles on and Ed runs with me for a few miles in the midday heat. We talk quietly about the challenge and share some memories as well as some hopes and fears. We even do a radio interview with one of the local stations. It all helps pass the miles and I'm definitely moving better.

Ashford and 65 miles and the crew keep the stop short. There is an air of urgency now: get him in, get sorted, and get out again: movement is good and static is death - so keep moving! On the couch in the shade, wipe down with baby wipes, cover head with wet cold towel, shoes and socks off, re-apply vaseline to feet, change socks, massage, shoes on - on yeah, and keep eating and drinking! Keep thinking GOOD THOUGHTS, you're getting there and everything's 'in the green.'

John has decided to run with me for a couple of miles - essentially to bully me into picking my knees up and opening my stride. He wants to see for himself what's happening out here in the field. I'm into my running quicker this time, and I'm immediately aware the pace is faster. So be it. I fix on John's heels in front of me and work to keep with him. "Work your arms - pick your knees up! C'mon Andy, work through it - it'll get easier as you get into it!"

So I grit my teeth and work as my world shrinks to feature the point between John's shoulder blades and little else. We're on a shit camber, the road has narrowed, and traffic is once again brushing past us. I'm trying to do 'relaxed' and 'flow' through clenched teeth. I'm aware I'm working way harder than previously and now my shoulders are aching with the effort. 'Just do it, man - don't think about it, just fucking *do it.'*

This time we don't stop after 2.5 miles. I try and remember that my world hasn't always revolved around chasing John's back, but this seems a pointless waste of mental energy, let's keep it in the present, shall we?

2pm and I collapse on the couch where the motorhome is parked up in a village hall car park. I'm breathing hard, in real pain and just want to sleep. John has run on ahead to get ready for me and tests a drinks bottle Charlotte has ready: 'That's no good, it's bloody warm - he needs something cold!' It's the first raised voice of the trip and reflects the urgency and concern John in particular feels as he works quickly to get to grips with my legs. Too quickly: his grip slips on my ankle, he falls forward onto me, my knee goes through full range of motion and I scream as the quad muscle is forced to full stretch. Jesus Fucking Christ!! I've tears in my eyes as I'm wrenched from the twilight zone into full wakefulness. John is suitably chaste, we all take a deep breath and settle down.

"I think that's 75 miles, Andy." Really? Where did that last few miles go then - I'm sure I've not lost track that badly - have I? 75 miles. Wow - that's close, I can almost touch it...

"Let me check that," says Eddie. "It may not be: let me check it." He knows that because of the detours the van made through London, the clock mileage in the van is slightly more that I have actually covered.

"Andy, that's 70 miles, 70 miles, buddy. Well done."

70 miles. I thought 75 sounded a bit far. Still, only 15 and a bit to go. I allow myself a smile as the crew go into serious pamper-mode. John is still working to keep the stops short, Charly is assisting with foot massage and vaseline while multi-tasking with food and text messages and EVERYONE is making a real effort to keep conversation going and talk the achievement UP: silences are not helpful right now.

After half an hour I'm off walking again still with John for company. I walk fast and try repeatedly to break into a jog but my legs are having none of it. This is fucking crazy - COME ON YOU BASTARD - RUN! You can move so you can run - come ON! Through silent tears of frustration which are fortunately indistinguishable from sweat I eventually force myself into a parody of a run - but it's NOT walking and that's ALL that matters.

It still feels fast though as John continues to run ahead checking over his shoulder periodically. My world has reverted to the familiar but now it's even smaller. I'm pretty much ignoring John, letting his exhortations pass through me, and just concentrating on MOVING FORWARD.

And then we pass the first sign I can remember with Folkestone on it. Folkestone's near Dover, isn't it? John's clearly delighted and I grimace in what passes for a smile in response. It's getting harder to keep running and I am reduced to a walk on the broken, narrow and overgrown pavement sections before cursing myself into running once again. Part of me is aware that a few red lights are starting to flash, and that part is trying to get the attention of the other part. Fuck off - can't you see I'm busy here?

Then the van comes into view and I wobble gratefully down the slight dip, stop, sway - and would have fallen if Ed had been less aware. He is able to catch me and lowers me into the shade at the back of the van as I'm finally forced to pay attention to those flashing red lights... Shit. This is definitely not good.

I'm now paying for those last miles with John with interest, and for a few minutes feelings of failure and frustration and helplessness overwhelm me. I can't stop the tears as I try to explain to Ed how I feel and why I'm crying. I'm still emotional when after some drink and fruit I set off walking again this time with Ed for company. I get it together fairly quickly after that though and Ed goes on ahead to leave me to walk the couple of miles or so to the motorhome at 75 miles. By the time I reach the crew again I'm composed and am walking strongly - but it doesn't last.

Once on the couch again surrounded by the guys the façade shatters. I have realised in the last mile or so that I CANNOT run any further. It's got nothing to do with anything else except that my quadracep muscles are shot and I physically cannot lift my knees any more. Feelings of failure and frustration simply swallow me. Seeing Charlotte tips me over the edge - I can't look her in the eyes so bury

my head in to couch and cry my eyes out. She reaches for my hand
and I know she's crying with me. A small part of me has registered
that everyone else has backed off and Tim is no longer filming.

"Babe." I raise my gaze and we smile at each other through the
tears. "What's wrong? you've done great, you're doing SO well..." I
realise she doesn't get it so try and explain. "I'm OK - everything's
OK, it's just my legs, my quads are fucked and I can't run - I just
can't!"

"So just walk for a bit and see how you feel."

She still doesn't get it.

"But it's a RUN - I wanted to run it: I just wanted to run the whole
thing, that's all... and now I can't... I just can't..."

She smiles broadly as she quickly realises there's no major
problems

"Ohhh... is that all! Look everyone, he's human after all - Andy's
human!"

And perspective comes quickly after that. I need to change some
shit, but as Eddie C points out, I'm actually walking faster than those
last few running miles and the main goal IS to get to Dover in one
piece. I'm still well up on record pace and have got just over 10 miles
to go. I know from the last mile or so I can walk strongly, my feet are
fine and I'm so close now I can almost taste it.

If walking is all I have left then I'll fucking walk the rest of the
way.

From Eddies log: *80 miles on the van clock Andy arrives at the
camper 3.31pm. He had a couple of wobbly moments during the last
4 miles but recovered well as he walked on. He had a few tears when
we talked, but all in all seemed OK.*

*He is now laid on the bed being well looked after. The afternoon
sun has been very hot. That has played it's part.*

*I phoned the skipper of the boat and he has told me he will call
when he has the weather report. I said there is no way Andy will not
swim tomorrow, but he (the skipper) did not seem so confident.*

*At the massage table all around Andy praising him and boosting
his confidence. He recovers quickly once he stops.*

3.46pm and he is getting ready to leave. The decision has been made to walk instead of run to the next target: the walk looks good and strong - the determination is back.

Walking the last few yards into Dover with the crew, on the phone to a local radio show!

I reach Dover and the end of the first stage at 7.10pm after walking the rest of the way: 18.5 hours since I left London. In my heart of hearts it's all a little later than I wanted, but I'm HERE which is the primary aim and I'll take that. The walk in has been interesting in it's own way: I've had to walk backwards down one particularly short steep hill - the only way my legs could cope - we've had traffic hailing us as a result of local radio coverage, and Chris Osmond our pilot for the swim has come out to meet us in advance of tomorrow. There are two swim windows: the first in the early hours of the morning and the second at midday. It's my call and I only briefly consider the first. We're up on schedule, I'm out on my feet, and I need to repair the damage - so it's midday tomorrow.

There are hugs and handshakes all around as we do the obligatory photos bit at the end of the run.

I move with all the grace of an arthritic octogenarian into the motor home.

"Ahh, it's nice to stop - what time is it?"

"7 o'clock - you've only been about 19 hours: NINETEEN hours - that's endurance, man!" John shakes his head in admiration.

"A little less, actually," corrects Charlotte. "It 's more like 18 and a half."

"18 and a half..." I'm a little slow as the effort of speaking is almost too much now. "Well, I couldn't go any quicker..."

The guys are quick to pour cold water on that one;

Charlotte "You flew!"

John "It was brilliant!"

Charlotte "Could you not? Really?!"

John "Perhaps the next time you'll be a bit quicker now you've got the hang of it!

I give in and have to smile. "Yeah - just a bit of a trial run, that..."

I realise that I am absolutely shattered, and once the smiles stop it's all I can do to keep my eyes open. The urge to just STOP, close my eyes and just lie down is nearly overwhelming, and the guys have to physically prop me up and steer me into our B & B for the night. Thankfully it's a ground floor room - but there is no bath! I can barely bend so the prospect of a shower is seriously daunting but somehow I manage. John comes in to do his stuff on my legs once again and we send out for ice-bags to speed the recovery. Apart from the traumatised quads I realise that I'm in quite serious pain in my right hip as well. The bursae is seriously inflamed to the point where I can hardly move. I definitely don't want to take this into the swim with me.

The boys are sorting themselves out but Charly and I are not going anywhere and eating in is the only option. She is shattered herself and is nearly reduced to tears after futile attempts to get some sort of takeaway food delivered to the B & B. I can barely string a coherent sentence together so she is forced to get this sorted herself and in the end has to go back out and buy a pasta takeaway to bring back. In the meantime I have fallen asleep and she has to wake me to eat. Barely has the last mouthful passed my lips and I'm out once again for the count and sleep like a dead thing all the way through to morning.

Performance is Emotional

Training is physical - Performance is much more about heart and soul. If it matters it will therefore hurt to fall short and all the 72 mile point illustrated was that IT REALLY MATTERED to be able to run the whole damn way. If you go back to how I set this up, the quality of the Journey is AS important as the Outcome. So my private goal, the one closest to my heart, had to be to commit to try to run it all. I didn't know if I could but there really was only one way to find out.

But there was always something to grab a hold of: multiple goals on many different levels and all within the various bite-size chunks meant that there was always some achievement to celebrate - and this was key in maintaining momentum. The pit-stops were also an opportunity to reflect and with time comes perspective - and I didn't need long. Physically I was in great shape so the physical recovery was fast, and we'd also set the stops up to maximise ALL aspects of the recovery, physical, mental and emotional. As Eddie noted in his log - I recover well when I stop. Mental rehearsal during the training meant that I'd worked on anticipating as many different scenarios as possible and was able to see myself dealing with each of them - the result? Not much took me by surprise!

The bottom line? Just get to Dover - and do it without killing yourself. In this context then the strategy was straightforward. Not getting the result I wanted? Learn from that QUICKLY and change the approach - but then get back on the horse and stay with it. Remember the Goal, the WHY of all of this and how far you've come already.

You must do that which you think you cannot.

The BBC finally catch up with us as we collect the motorhome from Brown-hills, Newark. "So can you tell us 'Why' Andy?"

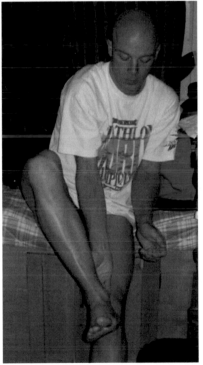

With Eddie Ette seconds before the start. So you're smiling now...

Last minute preparations at Marble Arch. TLC for my feet!

Nightime running through London

With Eddie Ette at the 50m point. A full kit change helps the re-charge.

Leaving Maidstone heading for the 50m point.

"Mummy what's that man doing?" John does his thing at one of the many scenic roadside stops

Above:
One stage down and two to go, a very welcome sight!

Right:
John does his thing on the couch in the Dover guesthouse

Below:
At least Charly and Eddie Clarke are enjoying it all

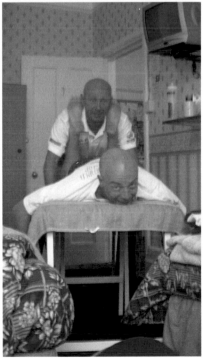

Above:
*The Crew at Dover:
(From left to right) Eddie Clarke; Charly;
Me; Eddie Ette; John Williams. (Tim Jury
on camera duty)*

Above:
*Eddie and Charly plan ahead
for the French bit.*

Right:
*Thank you Soreen! Charly
Eddie and I sampling the
sponsors product.*

Waiting

"The toughest thing for an athlete is competing in life when there is no more clapping"

Tom McNab, Coach and Author

Thursday, 18th September

The sun is shining and so are we. The breakfast table banter is in full swing as the success of yesterday and a night in a soft bed have set us all up for The Big One later on today. My hip has responded to John's treatment and my style of locomotion is looking progressively less like that of an arthritic giraffe!

At just after 8 o'clock Ed's phone rings. It could be anyone of a number of people, but we all watch and listen anyway while still shovelling breakfast down - and grow suddenly quiet as Ed's face falls. It's Chris our pilot who drops the bombshell, the swim is off.

The first reaction is amazement - it's a beautiful day out there! Then Ed points through the window to the flags we can see flying from the top of Dover Castle. "See those flags? Look at the way they're blowing - horizontal with the backs being whipped up. That means it's a Force 5 or 6 out in the Channel... THAT'S why Chris has rung!"

Bugger. That's really torn it, then. Eyes are looking towards me now as the news and it's implications are starting to sink in - but I'm looking at Ed "So where does that leave us?"

"Down at Chris's boat at midday" replies Eddie. "We have a meeting"

So midday finds Eddie and I in conference with Chris.

Chris: "I was on the 'net this morning looking at the forecast which said that the winds are going to go from 5 to 21 mph. I could see the weather coming in on the chart. The shipping forecast is Force 4, 5 and 6 - hence my advice that we don't swim today. They're saying no change for 12-24 hours, so we've just got to review it and take it on a suck-it-and-see basis. These can be wrong and these can be right: this is the difficulty you've got. I want to see the BBC forecast at 6 tonight, which I'll then marry with the stuff on the net."

"So we need to speak tonight and gear up for a 3 am swim." In my mind I'm calculating the hours.

Eddie looks up from his study. "But the chart doesn't show extreme weather here..."

"No, but the wind funnels between the two landmasses here so the forecast can be wrong - the Straits exert their own influence," replies Chris.

"What are the implications of that for swimming?" I need clarity here before we get lost in nautical-speak.

"Well, the air takes the easiest route over the sea as opposed to over the land," explains Chris. "If it's a northeasterly the wind is funnelled down the Straits and if it's a southeasterly it's funnelled up."

Ed looks across "Yeah - better for us if it's a southeasterly as it means it's more or less behind us when we're swimming. The bottom line is simple: if it's a Force 4 it's unswimmable over a long period. In short burst's it's OK - like we've done in training. I'm just glad we chose not to go at 4 o'clock this morning - if we had we would have abandoned by now, the weather's changed so much in a few hours this morning. He pauses. "The trick now is that we don't harass the pilot and we don't harass each other, just chill."

Chris grins and looks at me. "Yeah - I suppose Andy could do with the rest!"

I'm not arguing with that one and I've put the World Record option to bed already. "Hey - it's all bonus recovery time right now!"

Chris wants to be clear on our options and how long we can afford to wait. "How long do we have?" He's seen a big high pressure system on the forecasts due to come in over the next few days which is good news for us. "How long can you guys wait?"

"We can wait," replies Ed. We may lose some support but we're at the start of the tide so we can do it.'

I want to reassure Chris that he's not dealing with a muppet and I really am cool with all this. "We've trained together all summer - we've done the work and we know what I can do. It's all bonus time now so as far as I'm concerned we wait to get the best conditions. The more time we get the better it gets for me."

"You saw what I went through." Ed looks at Chris as they remember his own Arch to Arc swim where Chris was the pilot as well - 17 hours and nearly 30 miles in the water - the last part in darkness in a Force 5. "Andy's got the character to stick it out - but I'd rather we not swim on bad water!'

I'm beginning to learn this is all normal Channel swim 'let's-second-guess-the-weather' stuff and flapping about it is very, very pointless. Phoning a friend is not an option here.

I've rehearsed this and it's not jaw-dropping stuff, I say "All I'm asking myself is how can I use it to my advantage?"

And it really is that simple, I'm dealing with it so the rest of the crew is fine too.

Focus on what you can control, right?

From Eddie's diary
The meeting went well with Chris. We hope to swim at about 4am tomorrow. The wind is very strong now - I am not optimistic that we will go. Andy is very cool, calm and knows all you can do is wait...

Later that morning we head for the cliff tops overlooking the bay. While we are too high to see the waves clearly it is SERIOUSLY windy up here. Charlotte looks right into the camera as Tim is filming "I am sooooo glad he's not going in this - it's soooo windy!!!"

We have a Council of War later that evening back at the B & B. Chris has phoned earlier to say we won't be swimming early on Friday morning either. Its another bombshell in a series of bombshells, so we have been forced to take stock to keep the challenge on the road.

Eddie re-caps "Well, the 3am swim is definitely off as the wind has not abated at all. Chances of a 4 o'clock swim tomorrow? Well, maybe, but if any bad weather comes in dealing with it at night will be very tough. You'll be swimming through the night and a night swim is definitely more stressful for everyone. If it's bad we'll have to put a spotlight on you the whole way."

I remember my one night practice swim off Weymouth about 3 weeks ago on a eerily calm sea and I learned quickly then that I hate spotlights when I'm swimming, it completely buggers your night vision and any spatial awareness you have. The prospect of some 10 hours of spot light in an inhospitable sea is really not funny...

"Chris will call it at 8 tomorrow morning" Ed continues, "though I know he'd prefer not to do a night swim in dodgy weather."

"OK." I gather my thoughts. "Let's deal with the practicalities of a 24 hour delay, time and diary commitments for everyone..."

"Well, I can stretch till Sunday." Eddie C once again shows that nothing is too much trouble. I smile to myself as that's just the Eddie I've come to know.

"It would help," I say slowly, "if you would all forget any obligation you may or may not feel to see this thing through, let's just deal with the practicalities for the moment."

"Well the first thing is the worst case scenario." says Ed, "which is that there is no swim on this tide - which ends early next week. The second thing is - how long can YOU wait, Andy?"

"There are two considerations: we only have the motor home till Wednesday..."

"And that's a whole new set of problems if we have to extend that," jumps in Charly.

"That's the only barrier for me," I reply. "The second consideration is my dear wife - and for Charly it's a whole different ball game."

"It actually is possible for just you and I to finish this" Ed is still on worse case. "If everyone else goes home we can still complete if we get the weather."

A pause while this sinks in.

"For me, the chance of the World Record has gone." I'm speaking slowly and getting everyone's full attention now. "I'd be lying if I said I wasn't disappointed by that. But it was always the best case scenario and dependent on so many things out of our control.

The public face is that every delay is money in the bank, recovery time and all that - and that's all true BUT... But the challenge for me is to put it all together as closely as physically and mentally possible, That's now gone so a big part of the challenge is a little diminished for me. BUT I can accept that and shelve it because to do the whole thing is still a big pull - it's just not quite a big a pull as 'let's-do-it-when-WE-want-to-do-it!" Another dramatic pause. "I'll still take that though. If I have to sit and wait I will take that and do it to the best of my ability: that's the next level and the next opportunity I have."

We'll, that sure sobered everyone up!

Ed is nodding with an understanding which only comes from having done this thing. "That is the event" he states. "It took me three years because the weather is the governor and the Channel is fickle. The best in the world have failed - the best in the world - and you were definitely capable of beating my record - but I was definitely capable of going 20 hours quicker had the weather been with me! So here we are with the first two attempts delayed by the weather, though it looks like your wait will be longer than mine. I know EXACTLY what you're going through, and it takes a certain strength to say 'I'll continue with this.' You're saying that you will and I think you should, you'll still be only the second person ever to do it and THAT'S still a heck of an achievement. The World Record is a nice little addition - but it's only ever that in my opinion.

But what about everybody else?"

Tim: "I can stay. I've set my life up to do it - I'm fielding all sorts of personal conflicts but I can do it, but I want to say something here, there's a lot of very frustrated and ambitious people sat in front of me who I like an awful lot. We've achieved a great deal already - far more than I ever thought - and we can do so much more with this as a promotional experience. So I'd like to continue - 'cos I'm amazed at how good the footage is that we're getting and I only picked up the damn camera two days ago! But I also agree with Eddie: just to do it is an achievement." He looks over at me. "I understood you were competitive from the early days - but I also think that the next 5 people who do this will have these problems. One may get lucky, but you may find that what we achieve here still stands - and hey! I really think that we should publicise the split times - 'cos what you did yesterday stands out big time for me!"

Ed is nodding agreement "Yeah, that'll happen - but I'm pleased to hear Tim will stay 'cos I haven't got the skills to help you sell this. I threw away my chance 'cos I couldn't be bothered to get changed and put my rubber suit back on and pretend I'm doing it for TV! A massive mistake. You're promoting my business for me and I want to see you do it. But I will walk away tonight if you said 'I'm a little busy - I can't really afford to wait...'"

"And another thing," chimes in Tim, "Is that we've just learned an awful lot about how to run people 87 miles. You've done it once. Now you may choose to come back and have another go - I suspect you will - but by doing the next two legs you have the whole experience stacked away and THAT gives you options for a fast run in the future."

I decide to contribute some perspective at this point. "Hey, don't get me wrong, completion is a big thing. If we have to sit here till the end of the swim window, I'll take that. My frustration lasted for no more than about 2 minutes after Ed got the call from Chris. It always was the cream on the top - to go for it on MY time scale - so I couldn't and didn't dwell on it, it was just one of those 'wouldn't it be really cool if...'"

Tim's watching me carefully. He nods. "I know. You're a competitive athlete..."

"Of course, there's a whole range of emotions which go with that... but I'll take the opportunity to finish it off." I look over at Charlotte. "We've invested too much to walk away!"

"You like the phrase *big & hairy*..." at this point the room dissolves in laughter as Tim struggles to get his teeth in! He's clearly been spending far too much time among people who shave their legs...

Tim tries again. "We're treating swimming the Channel here as routine. It's not. It really isn't. If you go on and do this only THREE DAYS after that run it'll impress a helluva lot of people - and a lot of Channel swimmers at that! Just complete the thing, OK?"

"It's just big," Ed comes in, "too big for many people to grasp. That 87 mile run showed you just how big it really is - 'cos you didn't achieve what you wanted to. Don't underestimate the Channel - and I know you're not 'cos you've proven to me in training that you can do it - but just know that the best in the world have failed 'cos this got too big for them."

How do I get across that I KNOW this is mine without sounding like an egotistical maniac? I give it a shot "Look." The pause gets everyone's attention. "I'm not treating this as a done deal - really I'm not. BUT. We've done the work and I believe absolutely that we can do it. That's all. That's why we're talking about a Channel swim like this now when 4 months ago it was nowhere."

Tim again "I just want you to know that I think you should do it - I'll be ecstatic if you do!"

Heads turn to look at the lady in the room. "I want him to do it."

Charly is adamant as I knew she would be. "I think the opportunity is still there." She puts her hand on my knee and looks straight at me and grins "You need to do it!"

"I agree." Eddie flicks through his weather notes. "Looking at it all, it's lows all the way then high pressure over the UK at the weekend. Even if we didn't swim Saturday or Sunday you will still get a swim on this tide as late as Wednesday…"

"Finishing would be nice for the sponsors too, don't forget…" adds Tim.

"For myself, it would be easier to gear up for 24 hours from now than 4am tomorrow. All this 'we're-going-no-we're-not' lark is starting to wear on me now, and the prospect of more is not something I'm particularly looking forward to. I'm on an emotional roller coaster as it is so if I can do anything to bring some moderation to the party I will - and Chris has clearly said he feels we'll have a better chance in 48 hours time."

Ed is quick to pour cold water on that one. "What you've got to do is not get excited. We either swim or we don't. The only time you want to get excited is when we're actually on the boat. Remember I told you about my swim?" "Yeah, a bloody epic, that one…"

"When I went I couldn't get Tom down here. I had a choice, 5.30 or 9.30. 9.30 Tom could get here. At 5.30 I'd have 4 more hours of this little weather window. As it turned out it blew up much faster than that so I didn't get the weather with me but at the time I had to decide - so I had a complete stranger feeding me 'cos I went for the window. You need to be ready for every chance - don't discount anything just 'cos it might work out better for you."

And of course I know he's right. I need to be ready for every and any opportunity to swim. But it's still a slightly sobering thought…

Friday, 19th September

We spend much of Friday listening for the phone, trying to be cool and calm about everything and interviewing each other in front of the camera while parked in the Marina. Here's a few snippets:

Andy "Well, they say that behind every man is a stunningly

attractive and extremely capable lady… and that's absolutely true! So why are you here, Charly?"

Charlotte "I guess it goes back to February. I know you enjoyed the Chesil Challenge, (Eddie's 3 day triathlon challenge where we met him for the first time in September 2002) and that this had been in the back of your mind. But then you sat me down and said 'I've been thinking… I really want to do this!' I took a deep breath and said 'OK, tell me what it actually involves.' So I sat and listened for a while, looked at you and said 'Give me a couple of days and I'll get back to you on that one!'

'We talked at length afterwards and at the time you said that if we do this we do it together, we do it as a team because neither of us will have a good year otherwise. I had no real idea of what it would mean. I'd supported you at various ironman triathlons but those were a days worth of effort and we were talking more like a week here! What became clear was just how much was involved and just how much of our time it took, but we worked hard at that and made sure that we had time for ourselves so that you weren't training all the time. We had downtime together and it's worked out really well - time has flown and here we are!"

Andy "I remember that a key for you was that you wanted to meet Eddie Ette as soon as possible. Why was this so important?"

Charlotte "Well…" (pause and smile) "it's a pretty lunatic event! and I needed to see quite how much of a lunatic this guy was! So that first time in Portland in May I walked the beach with Eddie while you swam, and we sussed each other out. I realised he knew what he was doing and if I was going to entrust you to anyone I figured he'd be OK and when I met Lynne his wife, well I KNEW it would be OK!"

Andy "That'll be that woman-to-woman thing, then."

Charlotte "Well, she has been there and done it all before…"

Andy "She's also a Channel swimmer herself."

Charlotte "That's right, it was really sobering finding ourselves at dinner that weekend with two Channel swimmers - 'happens all the time!"

Andy "We knew at the outset that there'd be some great bits and some difficult bits with the preparation, never mind the actual attempt - and we talked about this a lot. I remember one particular conversation after my 10 mile swim between Weymouth and Lulworth which had not gone particularly well, shall we say..."

Charlotte "Ah yes. The big thing for me was to enjoy the process. I didn't want to live with a basket case for 5 months while you trained for this. I don't enjoy seeing you mentally beat yourself up for what you see as a poor performance, so after that swim we had to go back and remind ourselves WHY we were doing this."

Andy "I was a real basket-case, wasn't I? I remember coming home doing a Mr Caveman-short-tempered-woe-is-me husband impression! I was really down. The preparation was really hard and I was really struggling. I remember you saying to me 'Look. You're in a unique situation, you're swimming off the Dorset heritage coast in beautiful weather, so the least you can do is to try enjoy it! Look at the scenery, anything, just lift the mood! It's a position you will probably never be in again, so enjoy the opportunity to be there and take as much out of it as you can."

Charlotte "What you were losing sight of was just how much your emotions were affecting those people supporting you.

'We're all really supporting you, we want you to be successful - we don't want you to be unhappy, so to have you being down was really hard."

Andy "I remember that it was at that point that we really started to notice that there were an awful lot of people rooting for us, and because I'd been so wrapped up in the physical and mental hardship of the training I'd actually completely blanked that part out. You really helped me see the Big Picture at this point! It was almost after this conversation that we started to talk about 'so-an-so has been talking to me at work,' or we'd get a card or an email through. Suddenly we realised that there were a whole load of people out there who might have thought that we were really stupid (!) but were rooting for us anyway.

'You remember the Book of Advice?"

Charlotte (smiles) "Oh yes! An entire class from Manorfield Primary School where you help some of the kids with their reading! They'd spent their last afternoon of the term thinking up advice for you for the challenge and putting it together in a book with pictures they'd done, simple things but it meant so much. We were both a little damp-eyed when we read that, it was very, very special."

Andy "Kids call it as they see it, to them it's really simple so there's stuff in there like: *When you're doing it, try your best* and *Just think about the people that love you.* Of course it's all so true but easy to forget when you're wrapped up in the challenge of doing this thing. It really helped lift the whole mood and remind us why we were doing it.

'But then there are some very practical things which you are doing on this trip which help bring it all together..."

Charlotte "Well, I made sure you got fed which, over an 18 hour run was quite a lot of work to make sure it was all going in! We needed to make sure that you were fed and watered before you actually needed it. If you were asking for it it's probably too late.

'That was quite easy because we'd prepared for it. What I hadn't anticipated was all the other stuff! As we got closer to Dover the media interest was growing, as was our band of virtual supporters which were staying in touch by phone and text. The speed which that grew just blew me away! I was texting about 20 people to start with, who were then texting their friends who'd then contact me and ask to be put on the text list! Another friend started to put email updates out for us as well which meant that a whole load more folks could monitor your progress - and it's REALLY nice. Every time a message of support comes in I can tell you at your next stop. It's these little things which are enough to lift you - and the rest of us - and keep you going.

'I also made sure we were all branded up with our shirts, the motor home with it's boards and stickers, all little things I could do which meant you could concentrate on the *doing* part. So we look at all of what we've got and think 'hey - that's really good!"

Andy "Yeah, we've done pretty well! (Pause). Now I know that we've rehearsed this scenario - the weather delays etc but... how have you found the waiting, Charly - really?"

Charlotte (Leans back and smiles). "It's frustrating! I can't tell you just how much I wanted it to be the way you wanted it to be, eight hours rest and we're into the Channel! But you're such a good role model *focus on what we can do'* and that makes it easy for me. There's no point dwelling on the frustrations so let's focus on completion - and that's what we're going to do!"

Andy "So, the next couple of days, and we're due to start the swim tomorrow morning, what are you particularly looking forward to?"

Charlotte "I'm looking forward to the swim - it's a massive part of this challenge! To have a husband who's swum the Channel is pretty cool - but to have a husband who's swum the Channel AFTER an 87 mile run is very awesome... and then getting to Paris! It's going to be superb and I know we've worked for it..."

Andy 'Yep, I'll go with that!"

Charlotte "...and you're gonna do it!"

Andy "That's the general intention, and the odds are looking better and better all the time."

Later that afternoon back at the hotel Eddie clicks off his mobile from a call with Chris and looks me straight in the eye "Half past five down the boat tomorrow morning."

We are all gathered together and there's a exhale and a cheer from Eddie C while I pause to let it sink in.

"Good." I'm nodding slowly hands clasped nervously in front of me as I do reflective for a few seconds then, "Great! Let's get this show on the road!" I share a look with Eddie as resolve and respect for this next part slowly bubbles to the surface and I quickly quieten down.

"Alright. That's excellent."

"It's not gonna be an easy swim, I'll tell you that." Eddie's still looking right at me.

"No, well - it's not been an easy run," I reply.

Eddie C looks over at his namesake "He's got to work for this one."

Eddie nods slowly. "Yeah, well, let's hope it's not going to be too tough - but you're well rested and I'll think you'll need it..."

Later that evening in the restaurant we're all enjoying a last chance to relax before The Big One and as the evening draws on the rest of the crew enjoy the verbal cabaret which the two main protagonists thoughtfully provide...

Eddie "I just need a target, that's all..." A pause and a mischievous smile as the glass of wine is raised.. "And the Arch to Arc I don't need any more - 'cos I've already done it!"

Andy "Well, I knew that was coming!" The laughter dies down. "But you reckon you can do it in 60 hours, don't you?"

Eddie "Oh, I can. I can - no doubt about it!"

Tim "All the macho bullshit's coming out now - it's just great!"

Eddie does mock-serious "No, 60 hours is a very reasonable time to expect. Seriously."

I'm ready for this one, though and wait a few beats. 'I know, but 50's better."

As Charlotte nearly chokes on her wine Ed and I get into the inevitable 'how high do you wanna go?' routine.

"Yeah. Absolutely. 48 hours is the potential. Definitely. Look, realistically if you hadn't 'lost the wheels' as you call it, you'd have been down here in 14 to 16 hours. A rest? 4,6,8 hours? That's 22 hours. A 12 hour swim? 34 hours..." He shrugs because he knows he doesn't have to spell the rest out to me - I've done the maths myself weeks ago. So I do my own Marlon Brando-esque shrug.

"I know. 50 hours is on, I know it."

"I know you know." This wine is really good stuff! "That's why you're here 'cos you're a serious contender. The only anomaly is..." and here Eddie points knowingly at the ceiling, "what you've had to cope with and what I had to cope with, the weather."

He shares a conspiratorial glance with Eddie C and amidst rising hoots of derision "But I could beat him across," he looks over and winks at me "...I'm just not sure that I want to!"

Ah, the playground really is a beautiful place to be! We get serious again as Ed leans in.

"You gotta want to do it - yeah. And if I gotta want to do anything I'd rather do something else instead of the Arch again. But I really want to see you do it. If there's someone I'd like to see beat the record, I'd really like to see you do it." Shrugs. "But hey - the weather had other ideas!"

It was just the perfect way to spend an evening and take all our minds off the tension of the waiting and the anticipation of the morning. The standard of conversation however, wouldn't have won us any prizes...

Andy "That last training swim of mine was also significant in that finally, the pretence was off as to what the training swims were actually all about!"

Eddie nods sagely. "Ah - at last! The swimmers' perspective!"

I'm really into this game now. "Three hours pootling about, remember? That was the time when Tom..." a pause just to make sure I really do have his attention, "erroneously intimated that perhaps - just maybe, I might just have been swimming better than you were at that point."

It's getting increasingly difficult to hear ourselves speak amidst the heckling from the rest of the crew, but Eddie tries to get a good one back anyway. "You know, that's just typical of me - I blank out all the bad stuff and just file it away!"

"But I don't blank it out for two reasons." It was just hard to keep a straight face now, but who cares! "That was one of the reasons - the other one was that finally it became clear to me that all these training swims were, were just glorified fishing expeditions for you and Tom!"

Ed does quite a credible impression of 'the light dawning...'

"Yes... I do seem to recall you mentioning this at the time..."

"You weren't even trying to pretend otherwise! It was like, Oh, hi Andy - here for a swim? OK, just sort yourself out... now where did I put those rods..?!"

"You know what did it don't you?" Eddie clearly thinks an explanation is worth it at this point. "When the old fella was with us on the 8 hour swim he caught a sea bass - so Tom was absolutely adamant that he had to catch a bass as well! So that's what we had to do - sod the swimmer! So if Andy's got to come along that's OK, but we're going out to where we think the bass may be!"

"And I was swimming into fishing lines, getting tangled in all your stuff - and I'm like, 'What's going on?' And all I got was, 'yeah, yeah -

you know the score by now, just get on with it we've got some serious fishing to do here!'

It was revealed for what it truly was."

"No, No..." Ed feels some positive spin is needed at this point. "What it truly was, was that we realised that you'd reached the level where we could do no more..."

"I had now clearly surpassed you in Tom's eyes..." Well, I couldn't resist that one but Ed is not to be deflected!

"No, no - you hadn't! What he actually said to me was... 'I'll tell Andy that he's swimming better than you, Ed, but he's not really. I'm just saying it to make him feel good - but you make out you're really upset by it...'"

"Yeah, that's all fine and plausible except for one thing.." Time, I feel for an Unrefutable Truth at this point. "I actually believe Tom is nowhere near as cool and as calculating as that and that's a slur on his blemishless character for you to even consider saying that!"

"Ah."

It was that kind of evening.

From Eddie's diary

The day has been well spent. The breeze got up again this afternoon and the sea looked horrible. Maybe it was best we did not go as planned. We are all more than prepared now to go tomorrow. My feeling is that we will go, but it will be long and hard.

I go to bed with plenty on my mind. All the forecasts show little to no wind. Let's hope.

Swimming

"Even though you might be feeling nervous, and you see your shirt moving as your heart beats, you understand that it's OK to feel nervous. People say that you can shut out the noise of the crowd but that's rubbish 'cos you can hear the crowd all the time - you just understand that it doesn't have to matter if you don't want it to."

Jonny Wilkinson, Rugby

Saturday, 20th September
5.30am Dover Marina

And so it begins. I've been up since 4am so I can take my time getting ready which is my habit. Some food, check the gear and the feeds which we readied last night, and talking quietly with Charly about the practicalities of the day ahead. Keep everything slow and calm: now is not the time to rush. I'm quiet, calm, resolute and nervous in probably about equal measure. But nerves are good, right? Nerves means it matters, nerves just tell you it's special.

Oh, it's special alright.

Eddie has gone ahead and is down on the boat checking the latest weather forecast with Chris. The rest of the guys are waiting in the motorhome: I'm walking slowly up and down the quayside looking over the water. It's calm, quiet and warm. On land that usually heralds a good day - but over the Channel? My thoughts are my own: I've learned not to second-guess this. We are all expecting to go, but Eddie has been gone for a while now...

'Concentration is the ability to think about absolutely nothing when it's absolutely necessary.'

I smile as I remember one of my favourite quotes - and I focus on doing CONCENTRATION.

Eddie's back but the body language is all wrong. I force myself to say nothing as the crew gathers round. Ed takes a deep breath:

"I spent a couple of hours on the waterfront yesterday and I was looking at the sea and it wasn't at all pleasant. It was swimable but it wasn't pleasant. And if it's not going to be pleasant for 12 hours you wont last the duration - I wouldn't, none of us would.

'You've got two choices. It's an awful lot of money (note: the fee for the pilot's boat was £1600.00). We're prepped up and ready to go - Chris is ready to go. He's saying it's going to be better than yesterday, and I'm not going to argue with that - it could be or it couldn't. His gut feeling is that it's going to be better, my gut feeling is that the way the wind's been all week since we've been here... I thought it'd be better yesterday afternoon but it wasn't... Well, I don't know - I really don't."

He pauses perhaps expecting a reaction but doesn't get one. I'm doing stoney-faced so Ed ploughs on.

"I can make the decision for you - if you want - but you as the swimmer, you need to make your decision. There's a real chance you can get across. There's also a very real chance you won't with the weather the way it is… It is building up to be better, but that's another frigging day in your life and people may have to start thinking about going home. But as I said to you before, we can still make it work even if we lose people - it can still run." Another pause.

"Talk to Chris. Listen to him 'cos there's always two sides to a coin, but be ready to make your decision."

Silence. I'm vaguely aware everyone is looking at me for a response. My turn then; let's get some clarity here. "OK. So as we stand at this moment he is prepared not to go?"

"I'm not sure." Eddie shrugs. He's trying to help but I'm sure he can see that my thoughts are spiralling down towards turmoil pretty quickly.

"He can't take money off you. He can be pissed off 'cos he's come down here but that's his job, for Chrissake. He can't take you out on water that's not good - and he's not that sort of man anyway, because we wouldn't be working with him if he was.

'If he says to you that in his opinion it'll be better weather than yesterday, he really means it - and he's not just saying it to get the swim off and to piss you off 6 to 8 hours into the swim."

I'm still not saying anything, but I'm starting to think along the lines of 'is this for fucking real?!'

"If you abort the whole thing you'll lose your deposit 'cos he's waiting for you and that's very kind of him. Some pilots will say 'in my opinion it's a good swim day and you're going.' I don't think Chris will do that to you. He could do - but I don't think he will."

I know that it's only Eddie's strong sense of duty which has meant he has laid it out for me warts-and-all. He wants me to know how he feels but THAT makes it crystal clear to me that he and Chris are interpreting the weather charts differently - which put's me between a rock and a hard place.

Ed knows it. "You can be too clever about these things - too much of a thinker about them…!" It crosses my mind that it's a very polite way to say OH, FUCK IT!! ... "And sometimes you've just got to go with your gut feeling and experience..."

And with that, there's really only one thing I can do. I have to hear this first-hand from Chris.

Reflections from Charlotte

I remember thinking as I was listening to all this, 'that's really helpful, Eddie!'

I was actually really tired and quite confused by what was being said, there seemed to me to be so many reasons to go, and so many reasons not to go. Almost a feeling that Eddie didn't want you to go but that you needed to talk to Chris.

I couldn't think a great deal about it as there was nothing I could do. I couldn't give you any meaningful support other than... whatever your choice would be I'd go with it - so it was difficult.

I was just concerned about your state of mind, and when you walked back up from seeing Chris in the boat it was so obvious you were upset, your posture, everything, and we all thought, 'Oooh no - NOT a happy bunny!' I had no idea what you were going to do - I'd have gone with whatever - but you dithered and were undecided and that's so unlike you. You looked lost - like you genuinely didn't know what to do.

And I was: I was absolutely lost. On the boat, Chris had been patient and clear - but called it just as Eddie had said he would. The situation I faced at half past five in the morning of the biggest swim of my life - and the crux of the whole challenge was this:

If I chose to swim and the weather behaved as predicted, there was a very real chance that the conditions would deteriorate later in the day to the point where it would be unswimable. That could be 4,6,8,10 hours in - we just didn't know. If that happened the challenge would be all over because I'd already made it clear that if the swim was aborted for any reason I would not ride the bike leg.

Chris thought the forecast was pessimistic - Eddie wasn't so sure.

We could, however, afford to wait. We still had opportunities to swim on this neap tide and the weather was predicted to improve over the next few days. Even if some of the crew had to return home we could still make this thing work.

But we were here, now - prepped and ready to go and we've already waited 60 hours.

'Wanna phone a friend?

It was a decision I simply didn't want to make, and I was in tears as I walked back with Eddie from talking with Chris. Tears because I just want to swim! Tears because this is hard enough as it is - so don't make it any fucking harder for me! The culmination of all the months' preparation, the experience of the run, the tension of the wait, and what was at stake here simply combined to overwhelm me. Make it all go away please, I JUST WANT TO FUCKING SWIM!

But in the meantime Charlotte and I simply stood alone on the quayside and silently hugged each other while I summoned the courage to decide.

I turn to Eddie. "OK. I'll go," I mumble. His response is immediate and shocking "Don't fuck about Andy, don't even think about it! You're either ready to go or you're not! This is the Channel, for Chrissake! If you go into this half-hearted you'll fail and everything you've done will be wasted. So either commit or don't but don't do both!"

But it has to be today - it has to be. I've known this since I woke up this morning; that little voice telling me that today is the day I swim the English Channel - I just need to start paying attention now.

I straighten up and look squarely at the bloke who I respect hugely and has almost invested as much as I have in all this. "No. I'm ready." A hint of a smile. "Let's go and do this thing." And while we talk some more in private this is simply a chance for both of us to reaffirm with the other. The bottom line for me is simply this - let the chips fall where they may. I can walk away with my head held high from a try - but it has to be today.

From Eddie's Diary
...Met Chris at the Marina office and picked up the days' forecast. To me it did not look good. I chatted with Chris and he seemed to think it could work.

Andy is ready. Keen to get the job done. I felt it my duty to tell him my feelings. They may be wrong, but that's how I felt.

After quite a lot of talk between all concerned we decide to go.

0625. Approaching the beach. We can see at least one swimmer about half a mile away already started. That is good and helps boost our confidence - maybe the correct choice has been made after all...

Reflections from Charlotte

You said you'd go, but I remember Eddie got quite cross and lost his rag a bit 'Don't fuck about - don't go if you're not ready!' because he could see what we could see: you hadn't decided - you weren't sure at all. Maybe that was him being perceptive or maybe he was just as frustrated as you, but it was enough to change you like THAT, and you said, 'No - I'm going'

It was weird - almost a change of attitude as opposed to a change of decision. You said you were ready but I could see your emotional state didn't reflect that - then all of a sudden everything about you changed, whether it was the fire from Eddie which made you do that, I don't know. It was just that none of us had ever seen you looking so lost - so everyone else was wondering what to do as well.

Once the decision was made it was easier for us all to know what to do - but I WAS worried! Everyone was worried. It was calm in the harbour, but outside? We didn't have a clue!

We were about to find out, but the immediate task was to keep out of the way as much as possible in the boat while Chris and his crewman Tony, (handily a local triathlete as well) readied the vessel for departure. There's still tension - and while Chris and Tony understand the reasons, we will be spending all day with them on a small boat - so good first impressions are vital.

At 6.15am we cast off and head out of the harbour to Shakespeare Beach.

My world shrinks down to the familiarity of my immediate pre-swim routine: I'm now operating exclusively in bite-size chunks and focusing on those things which I can absolutely control. I have completely blanked out the big picture as it's just not helpful: biggest swim of my life; hardest swim in the world; at least 22 miles and probably more given the currents; all day in the water; the possibility of bad weather later on... All these things are true but to dwell on them would put me in a box. And a box is where I've just come from!

I now need to be feeding a 'can-do, will-do, am-doing' mindset on a continual basis because how I feel will directly influence my performance in the water - and my actions and my mood will directly affect those around me. I know this from my work, my research and my own practice - so it's time to deliver.

I'm already wearing my wetsuit up around my waist. Designed for triathlon swimming, it's a made-to-measure Terrapin, with full arms and leg covering which I have almost swum to death - but it fits me like a second skin and doesn't rub - as long as I prepare properly.

I go through the first part of my warm up routine: circle the arms through all range of movement to get the blood flowing, then stretches for the back, chest, shoulders, neck and arms. Gentle ones first then building in range of movement and the length of hold. Finish with the frontcrawl arm action, bent over, relaxed and smooth then building the stroke rate.

The first task is to grease my upper body. Tops off, hand into polythene glove, gloved hand into vaseline tub. Under the arms, along the line of the lats, over and around the shoulders, around the neck, along the line of the chest muscles, into the crook of the arms and around the wrists. After all the training swims over the summer the suit is impregnated with vaseline which will eventually rot the material - though this has also helped beat the chafing risk. I figure it's got this one last swim in it though after which I will retire it with honours.

My focus is on doing the task properly. My thoughts are on what I have achieved so far and the challenges already faced and overcome. This is simply another one, and my track record with this shit is good...

We clear the harbour entrance. The sea is flat calm: no wind, clear sky. Charly watches me quietly from the other side of the boat and breathes a silent prayer of thanks that her first fear has proved groundless: the weather is with us - so far.

Eddie comes over and takes over liberally applying the vaseline all over my upper body, then helps me wriggle my arms into the suit and close the zip up my back. I have learned that I can tell immediately by the fit of the suit if it is going to rub - and this one won't. Secure the collar flap, sit down and pull on the neoprene socks - rolling the legs down over the sock tops. Stand up to a few experimental stretches to settle the suit once more: the next time I take this off will be on French soil...

Chris breaks my concentration with news via the coastguard that two pilot boats have already set off with swimmers attempting the Channel. This is good news and everyone visibly relaxes as we strain to catch a glimpse of them about a mile away. So other people think today may be a good day, then...

I stand at the rail looking out over the horizon. I can't see the French coast but that doesn't matter. I've decided that the two directions I won't be looking during the swim is ahead or behind me. No point, I'll watch the shipping, the guys on the boat, or the fishes in the big blue - anything else is just not helpful.

We're getting closer. I'm still at the rail, mind calm and clear just watching and waiting while the sights and sounds and smells wash through me. It's all very familiar now - almost comforting - so I see without seeing, and simply *experience* for a while...

"Look - it's Eddie Clarke!" Ed points to the familiar figure walking along the shoreline to intercept us. Eddie Clarke may just have the hardest job of all today. He will be waiting for our call when we are about 2-3 hours out from the French side so he can bring the motorhome over on the ferry to meet us at Calais. For now, he is walking along Shakespeare Beach to wave us off.

It breaks my mood, back to task. Ear plugs in, neoprene hat on and bright yellow swimming cap fit snugly over the top to cover my ears as well. My world goes quiet as the boat glides to a stop about 100 yards of the shore. Pick up my goggles, I've been using clear lenses for all my swims, and hold my noseclip temporarily between my teeth. I've kept my wedding ring on for all my training swims so far, but this time I've decided to remove it. Charly and I have a final moment together while I struggle to do just this! A smile, a look, and a kiss as she takes the ring from me, and then I move towards the back of the boat.

Goggles on. Eddie looks at me. "The clock starts when you leave the beach, so swim to the beach and then we start. Stand on the shore. When I drop my hand we start the clock, OK?"

I nod. "Is it deep enough to drop in here?" I'm peering over the back of the boat.

"Yeah, but use the steps at the back of the boat."

A handshake and a look is all we need: time to go.

Handshakes to Chris - "Alright, Boy!" - and to Tim who has been on camera duty all this time, "'Just a day at the office!"

Fit the noseclip and Eddie helps me climb onto the dive platform at the back of the boat. I check my bearings one last time "It's OK to dive?"

"Yeah - it's OK to dive" Eddie reassures me. A last look to line up on the figure on the shoreline...

Eddie pats me gently on the back "Go, Andy!"

And I'm in. The water feels warm as I swim gently to the beach. I climb out to say a last farewell to Eddie C; a look and a handshake once again and I turn away and wade back into the water as a whistle comes from Eddie on the boat, "Go!"

6.37am. Showtime.

Reflections from Charlotte

(From boarding the boat) I was trying desperately not to be a landlubber as we've got to spend all day with Chris and Tony and I really don't want to appear a muppet! It was good to see you were just getting on with your preparations...

As you were greasing up I thought it was nice to see Eddie come along and, in a very fatherly way start to help you. He was nervous too but these little rituals help settle everyone down - though I'm still feeling a little redundant at this point!

What a relief when we came out of the harbour and it was calm - and I was hugely relieved as well to spot the other pilot boats.

I did feel for Eddie Clarke when he left us on the quayside when we were still unsure - he'd be out of contact for a while and he obviously wanted you to succeed. I was surprised when you remembered to take your ring off and hand it to me - but it was nice... I was just working hard not to distract you at this point!

Half an hour in and I've settled into a stroke rate of 63. The water is 18 degrees with the wind SSW. Wave height is 0.3m, visibility 10km: dare I hope it will stay like this all day? Despite the fact that I've been out of the water for a few days, my swimming has come easily. I'm about 30 yards off the port side of the boat watching the sun come up and the ferry traffic in and out of the harbour. It's a stunning sunrise so I simply relax and enjoy the sight while keeping

Ed and Charly on the boat about an hour out. It's warm and calm but will the weather hold?

everything smooth and controlled.

I work hard at not anticipating the first feed. This summer has taught me that the first interval usually feels the longest, so chill, relax: the guys will signal when it's time. And sure enough at 7.20am I spot a silhouette in the back of the boat holding a feed bottle aloft, so I angle towards the boat and get ready the pre-feed routine: swim to the bow and allow the drift to take me down the side of the boat.

Tread water, goggles up, noseclip off and hand it up. Don't hold onto the boat! Smile, be nice, say 'thank you' for the bottle, lean back into the water and drink - making sure to finish it.

"Well done, matie!" Eddie is looking down as Charly dispenses refreshment. "Maltloaf?"

"Thanks." I wash a chunk down with the warm carb drink, multi-tasking like a good 'un. I know I need to keep these stops short. Even in 18 degrees every time I stop I cool down, and as the day goes on it will become harder to get going again. Even a 'fast' 12 hour swim will be about 16 stops - and that's a heck of a cumulative effect that I would prefer not to go down.

"John Williams has rung - and Philippa, your Aussie fan club!" Charlotte is smiling down at me. I vaguely remember she picked up a slightly confused voice message from Phil last night.

"Was she pissed, then?" I grin as I remember how bemused we were at the time.

"No - just emotional!"

"Yeah." Charly and I share a look. "It was that kinda night, wasn't it?"

Time for a last look at the early morning sun on the white cliffs behind me as I digest maltloaf, time to go.

Retrieve the noseclip, goggles on and kick away from the boat. Some dental hygiene - I have learnt that swimming with bits of malt loaf in my teeth really annoys me - a few strokes of backstroke to get going before a flip over to resume normal service. Total feed time 1 minute 20 seconds.

Ed talks to the camera while completing his log:

'I'm absolutely delighted. The sea is like glass - it's fantastic! After all the discussions this morning I was really worried that after the forecasts I'd seen there'd be no swimming. Andy is SOOO pleased - if this continues we'll be there in 10 hours: I'm sure of it. He's full of himself again, and that's exactly what we want. We're approaching the shipping lanes and he's flying!'

Was I ever! Everything felt good: smooth, symmetrical, powerful, relaxed. I could taste the speed and was simply relishing the opportunity to swim well in a tame Channel. As Chris was explaining to the guys on the boat... this was the variable bit while the wind decides what it wants to do: Currently it's misty, calm and pancake flat. Meanwhile yours truly was concentrating on getting as close to the French side as possible before the weather decided to stop being nice to us...

You hear the shipping before you see it when you're swimming. I'd got used to this during the Portland swims so it was no longer unnerving. The throb of the engines and the sound of propeller blades. Almost like the sound of someone sweeping a yard with a stiff brush... The wake of the SeaCat was another thing entirely, and even I could see that this one was pretty close off to my left and if the wake looked that big from this distance..! What I hadn't appreciated or rather just not thought about really that 'focus on what you can control' bit again(!) - is that the shipping *moves round* the swimmer. It's obvious, of course, but there is a strict hierarchy. Powered craft move round sailing vessels, and everything moves around us. Well, we are moving the slowest of the lot so taking evasive action is a bit fruitless really! There are stages in the 'no, you really are getting a bit close now, ' process as well. Radar and radio, coastguard to ship, ship to ship etc. It's when you notice the signal lights being used that you know it's really getting interesting!

The other indicator is watching to see how the pilot boat gets thrown around as the wake hits broadside on! Being in the water in a BIG sea means that as a swimmer I wasn't really aware of being caught - the waves are widely spaced and rolling - but to momentarily lose sight on the boat as we alternate between the base and the top of the wave trough is a pretty good indicator that the SeaCat was a little too close and a little too fast! Chris was certainly giving vent to his feelings in no uncertain manner!

Feed 4, 9.30am

"You must have been very righteous, I tell you!" Ed grins down at me as Charlotte hands me the bottle and the weather continues to bless us.

"Yeah" A loud gulp. I look up "Can't have been that righteous though otherwise we'd have gone two days ago!"

"You wouldn't have got across two days ago!"

I pause round my drink and offer up a wry smile: the man does have a point there... Ed catches my mood, "If only, eh? If only..."

"Yeah." I'm still a happy bunny whatever. "It's not bad, though!"

Charlotte brings us back to the present as I chew my way through a chunk of energy bar "Did you see the fish or the sea gull?"

I remember that my darling wife is also on Wildlife Watch, and I do remember being buzzed by a sea gull...

"Saw the sea gull, but fish - no!"

A quick stop this one, 75 seconds later I'm on my way...

Feed 6, 11.00am.

"A bit of traffic, then!" I grin round at the container vessel passing us about 400 yards away as Charlotte hands me a cup of fruit salad for a change. For the last few minutes all sorts of interesting things have been happening as said ship has been coming up close behind us and Chris has been on signal light duty before it altered course to avoid us - which was nice.

"Yeah - very entertaining!" Charlotte launches into a blow-by-blow account of it all 'Flashing lights and radioing people and waving at them and everything!" I figure she's having a good time. "You're aware of it all down there, then?"

Oh yeah! "You hear the propellers..." I start to explain.

"Is it loud?" she asks.

"No, it's like - how to describe it?" My explanation is interrupted by a loud fruit-salad and seawater flavoured burp. I give up. "I'm not sure... I'll get back to you on that one!"

Back to business: an expectant pause.

"It feels like I'm making good progress..." I look up at her hopefully. What I really mean is that I want to hear that I'm at about half way, I've broken the back of it and it's all downhill from now on. It's been going well but I have been pushing on and the first signs of tiredness are starting to surface. By the position of the sun I figure that the morning is pretty well advanced so that must mean... It's the first sign of cracks in the 'progress in bite-size chunks / focus on what you can control' mentality. I'm also starting to feel my hip aching from the damage done during the run, and I know how this could spread into the muscles around my pelvis and small of my back...

Charly is buoyant "You're making great progress - doing good, mate!" She smoothly shifts gears and her eyes shine. "Looking mighty fine!"

I can't help but smile around a mouthful of fruit salad and show my appreciation with another loud burp - oops! "Sure is a tasty fruit salad!" Charly still needs to work on her John Wayne impression. This stuff does seem to be making me burp rather a lot, though...

I turn to watch a ferry passing our port side, "Get out of my way!"

"They are doing - are you impressed?" Once more my wife is in ego-building mode "They're moving for you!"

She can read the unsaid stuff pretty well though and leans over to look straight at me as I take my noseclip from her. "C'mon babe, you're looking great - keep doing what you're doing!"

OK then. "Aye." A smile and a wink in return. "Back to the office, then."

Eddie talking to camera:

'He's doing very well indeed - very well. He's got the toughest bit to come - no doubt about that - but conditions are ideal and he's pushing on. It's all down to him...'

But it still felt good. With the tune of 'Onward Christian Soldiers' rolling round my head I went through Feed 7 at 11.45am with a two and a half minute stop and no problems, but I was having to work increasingly hard to stop myself asking for progress reports and to ignore the pain which was building in my hip. I'd started to flutter kick periodically to ease the cramp-like pain, and all the way through Feed 7 I stood vertical in the water doing a running on the spot action. It helped ease the hip - for a while.

Lots of things were still going right but the bottom line was now this, at nearly 6 hours in a few warning lights were starting to

Ed keeps score in his log.

flash...

Feed 8 at 12.30pm was the longest one yet, (three and a half minutes) which told it's own story.

Ed recorded in his log:

"He asked if he'd broken the back of it and I was quick to say halfway and no more. He needs to know lots to do yet... it will be interesting to see what he says when he comes in next... "

Ed had flattened me a little with this revelation - I'd really thought I was further on. Only half way - bugger! I'd had it pegged for nearer to 8 hours. I'd deliberately allowed myself to lose track of the feeds as I'd just wanted to lose myself in the swimming, no clock-watching, just keep doing it. But - Jesus! this hip hurts - and I've got this for another 6 hours at least. Fuck. Oh well, you won't get there by moaning, Mounce, so better get on with it...

So I did. But in the middle of the English Channel I was now beginning to feel just how big and scary this thing was. I'd done all the training on my own since the end of May, and while the crew had been with me from London, it was still just me at the business end. And it was just bloody hard! The training, the last bit of the run, the waiting, this morning - and now this: oh, and there will be more! I was just feeling plain lonely at this point, and though I didn't realise it at the time I was compounding the feeling by continuing to swim 50 yards off the boat. With the sun and boat to my right all I could see were silhouettes - they weren't real people. It was just little ole me in the big blue sea.

My world had shrunk to managing the growing ache in my hip a few strokes, the odd grimace, drop the head, flutter the feet, relax, relax, stay smooth. At times I actually stopped dead in the water as I brought my knee up to my chest and back while still horizontal in the water. Nothing I did seemed to help and in the end I was left with one strategy: fuck it - just get on with it! But I was swimming like I felt, the guys could see it and Ed took a stroke count to confirm it. I was down to 56. Finally, after what seemed like an eternity, I spotted the feed signal and made my way miserably to the boat.

Feed 9, 1.15pm

"Hello! Get a load of that!" Charly is as pleased to see me as ever and is pointing to a rather large passing container vessel. I couldn't give a shit at this point and she gets no answer as I just pull a face and swear under my breath. I'm breathing harder than normal and won't look her in the eye.

She's no dummy, "Want some ibuprofen?"

I finally look up "My hip's fucking killing me."

"I'll get you some." Charly is all business as Ed turns to help and I'm passed 2 tablets. The ethics of what I'm about to do go right out the window, I'm in serious pain, there's still a bloody long way to go, and as far as I'm concerned this is survival. OK, so I'd prefer not to have to do this, but lots of Channel swimmers use this stuff. Heck,

I'VE used it before and I know it works so just give me the damn
things, will you?

As the swell hits from the passing vessel I drop one of the tablets
"Don't worry" Charly is immediate, "I'll get you another one."

I get 'em down my neck like a good 'un.

"Do you want something to eat? What do you want? Powerbar?
Maltloaf?" Charly is still in "let's-just-bloody-get-this-sorted" mode,
but I can't, or won't make the effort to help her.

"I don't know - anything."

Oh, that's really helpful Mounce, but she passes me something
anyway.

"Andy." Eddie has been watching and listening intently. Part of me
registers that he is speaking slower than normal and has waited till I
look at him before continuing. "Are you feeling cool?"

I think about that one before realising that I'm shaking more than
normal and my teeth are starting to chatter.

"Yeah." I'm biting off the words and long sentences are just a plain
waste of energy right now.

Ed turns away. "Tony! I'll stick him round the other side, OK?"

Charly reaches urgently to hold my hand and looks right into me
"Just keep doing it - you're doing great, just keep doing it, OK? You've
just got to keep doing it - OK?"

She gets through and I remember that the painkiller will kick in
soon so just be patient for a while longer...

"Andy!" Eddie's back. "When you leave just keep swimming
forward and we'll drop back and come up on the other side of you
and you'll be in the sunshine, mate!" He grins at me. "Might as well
see it - it's lovely!"

The strategy is a good one and the positive spin is also starting to
register.

I finish my drink.

"Hold my hand." I reach up for Charly and the brief clasp between
us speaks volumes, then I'm away - but I've been 6 minutes which is
more than twice the average feed time so far.

Stay relaxed, slow down, swim close to the boat. Breathe to the left
more and watch Charly sitting up in the bow. Yeah, it feels warmer

already. Stay close in and give the tablets a chance to work. Smile at your favourite lady when you breathe...

And it's working, I'm feeling happier already. The proximity, the company, the sun on my back... we had to change something and we had to do it pretty fast. So now be patient, relax, and just see how you feel at the next feed, just get to the next feed and see... you can do this... smile, stay smooth... just get through this bit...

Feed 10, 2.00pm (7.5 hours)

"Alright, mate!" Ed hands me the feed.

"Better." The one word says it all and I have my Game Face back on. My stroke rate is still too slow (53-54) but I'm definitely through the worst.

"Good!" Charly has been looking down anxiously and hands me a special treat.

"Fruit - and a cup of tea!" Ed has also wisely changed strategy on the feeds. "We're not going to give you any carb drink this time..."

"Good!" I definitely fancy something different and the tea is to die for right now - how about some jelly babies as well? And sure enough they appear as if by magic and I take great delight in biting the heads off!

"You got a message from Ray & Leyshon - they must be racing today or something." I smile and nod as I remember our two triathlon friends from back home. Charly grins as she continues "They texted to say that they're stuck on the M42 and you're probably going quicker than they are right now! And Rachel & Mick texted: they said they're with you all the way - they're flying back from France so they'll look out of the window for you!"

It's a great moment: four friends who would never know how timely their messages were. If ever I needed a pick up it was right now - and I also know that this stuff is a tonic for the crew as well. People are still taking the time to remember us and I'm sufficiently together again to register that this makes it all just a bit more special.

So we all just grin at each other for a few moments while I continue to get the feed down.

"Charly." I realise what has been so helpful these last 45 minutes.

"If you sit in view periodically that's really helpful..." Being able to see and pull silly faces as I breathe to my favourite lady has worked wonders.

Charly knows it "Yeah - I'm going to... "

"The company's good, y'know?" It's a bit of a pathetic explanation but I figure she can fill in the gaps for herself.

"Yeah - I'll do that and go look at you!"

There is a danger of this becoming a husband and wife love-in, so as there are other people involved here...

"You can come as well, Eddie - if you want - so you don't feel left out!"

The reply is unprintable.

"Charly, you just sit in view, will you?"

"What, and do this?" She mimes a big smiley wave.

"Yeah - that as well, it just really helps, y'know?"

"Course it does!" Ed has been enjoying the last few minutes and more importantly he knows this stuff better than anyone else on the boat. "Here! Cup of tea!"

Hurrah!

"Still trying to get your bloody brother-in-law to make us one!"

No change there, then!

"Malt loaf, or anything?" Charly asks me.

I think about that. What the hell... "Got any Jaffa cakes?"

"And?" Eddie is doing slow and deliberate again, but this time it's not quite as serious:

"How-are-you?"

Time to have some fun here...

"I'm a bit tired... " I'm smiling round a mouthful of Jaffa cake.

"Why?" Ed has been practising ironic, obviously...

"And a bit wrinkled... Trying not to anticipate THE END..." I grin up at him. "Just knowing that we are getting there..."

"We are indeed." Ed has found wise-old-man-of-the-sea mode. "Every armstroke is a stroke nearer!"

"Philippa rang from Australia again!' Charly has clearly been in telephone exchange mode. "She's been to see the Sydney Sharks playing the Brisbane Bulls at Aussie Rules - and Brisbane slaughtered them! 71,000 people there - she really enjoyed it. But she said she was thinking about you all the time! She was trembling when she picked up the last text update 'cos she was worried - so she was really happy when it was good news!"

Shit - how can I not do this with all these folks rooting for us?

"Anything else to eat? No?' Charly retrieves the bottle from a well and truly re-vitalised husband. And all this in two and a half

One of Charly's tasks was to keep our virtual support crew up-dated. Here she texts out the latest news.

minutes...

3.30pm From Eddie's Log:

'Andy is well focused. Stroke looks good. Still very warm and I'm still sitting with my shirt off! Sea conditions still very good with a slight chop...'

Yeah: where was this bad weather we were promised? It's been a glorious day so far but conditions can change so quickly here. No one is relaxing just yet, but maybe the weather gods will continue to smile on us for this crucial last quarter...

It's a small world. Tony is on the radio talking to Dover coastguard. The desk is being manned by Nicky, one of the members of Deal Triathlon Club who had to abandon her own Channel swim attempt last year as part of a relay team due to sickness. This Channel thing is clearly just what you do down here to pass the time..!

At about four o'clock Tony does a piece to camera to give a positional update:

'We can now just about see the French cliff tops - and the Abbeville buoy which is about 4-5 miles away. The sea temperature is 18.2 degrees. Cap Gris-Nez is off to our right, down at our one or two o'clock. Normally we try and go straight to Cap Gris-Nez which is the shortest distance across. We try and steer 150 degrees and whatever the tides are doing they take us either up or down the Channel. Ultimately the swimmer is swimming across the Channel in that mass of water which is just moving sideways. Today we went 140 degrees because it was forecast to blow up this afternoon, and it was going to blow up from the east which meant it would blow us sideways to the west - so we compensated 10 degrees to make up for that. If it doesn't - and it hasn't so far - we'll be a little bit further east than is perfect, but this does mean that Andy has had an almost perfect day weather-wise in the water - which is far better for him! We think ETA at about 7pm which will give him about twelve and a quarter hours in total.'

Feed 13, 4.15pm

"Is it suitable to ask how long - or not?" I'm through the worst and have been watching the wave tops sparkle as the sun lowers itself to the horizon. It's just beautiful and I'm feeling very much at peace with the world. At this point, Ed could tell me nothing and I wouldn't care at all.

Ed looks at me. "It's very difficult to give you a time. VERY roughly - about 3 hours." He pauses to allow this to register. "The way you're chugging away at it, it shouldn't be any more than that, mate."

I do a hurried calculation. "Three to four feeds - ish."

"Ish" Ed knows the double-edged sword nature of absolutes at this point in the swim. He has told me horror stories of swimmers who get within a couple of miles of the French coast and then are forced to abandon after failing to make headway in the currents which get stronger the closer we get to the coast.

But so do I. "Yeah - I know, I know."

"Look, by that time you'll be fucking falling over the rocks if you ain't there!" Guess Ed is quite confident then… "And you'll be the last one to see the cliffs - they've all seen them already!"

I know. I've seen the guys pointing ahead as I've been swimming and have guessed what they have seen - but I'm still not looking that way myself yet…

The end is definitely in sight though, or as my wife puts it "You can see it - it's big - and French!"

We all have a smile about that one…

"It's going OK…" I realise the guys can see this but saying it out loud helps me as well - and it really is going OK.

"Brilliant." Which is Ette-speak for 'I'm really very pleased!' Then I spot that familiar glint in his eye as he grins down at me. "I don't know what to say though, 'cos you're not as quick as I would've been!" Here we go again…

"Cause, I'm not doing it in real conditions am I?" I DO like this game…!

"Christ, no!" Comes the reply from the owner of a 17 hour and over 30 miles of Channel crossing.

"It's swimming for poofs, this isn't it?!"

Guess spirits are quite high at this point, then! Back to the serious stuff, Ed is on catering detail for a change.

"Is there anything you'd like to eat? I'd just like to see you eat something more substantial, y'know - bread and butter?"

"A jam sandwich - with a cup of tea at the next feed?" I've no idea where that inspiration came from but now it's out it definitely sounds like a good idea!

"OK, we might have a bit of that…" come the reply from catering.

"Great!" I get ready to leave. "Back to the desk…"

"John Williams says 'get on with it!'" Charly is still doing communication nerve-centre.

"Hey." Ed looks straight at me. "They ain't got a clue."

"They haven't, have they." But it's still great to hear it.

"I'm sure if he was here he'd be running along side you!" laughs Charly.

I'm into my few strokes of backstroke "Go, Andy - go!"

Feed 14, 5.00pm

I'm happily washing my jam sandwich down with mouthfuls of tea and seawater - but it just tastes great! My hands are shaking quite a lot but I'm in good shape and am still sticking to my discipline of not looking ahead to landfall.

"2.7 miles from the shore." Chris is talking to Ed but I don't hear it.

"Good." Eddie turns to Charlotte "Got any jelly babies or something?"

Charly goes rummaging, "I have some jelly babies for my baby..!"and hands me some down.

"Thanks, but I'm sweet enough!"

"That bread will soak up some of the liquid..."

"Is that right?" Sarcasm is coming very easily now as we're all getting a little giddy at the prospect of THE END.

"I reckon." Ed also does deadpan really very well.

"What are you, some nutritional expert or something?"

"Course I am - that's why you're eating it!"

The boat is dissolving into laughter as the guys enjoy the impromptu cabaret.

"I 've got earplugs in, so I can't hear any profanities, you know..." Even I'm impressed at my ability to say such big words at this stage!

We're all just grinning at each other like idiots and I catch Eddie's eye as I get ready to leave "You want to be careful, or you'll get emotionally attached to your charges..!"

But it's way too late for that though.

Goggles on: "Right. Let's fuck off!"

But I don't, because as I turn I can't fail to spot a bloody great big cliff in front of us.

"There's a bloody big cliff over there!"

"That's right, mate!" Ed is smiling at the recognition. "Can you see it?"

"Fucking hell - it's huge!" I really am not kidding now and am genuinely shocked at how close we seem to be.

"It's where you're going. That's Cap Blanc over there - France!"

"Well it's about bloody time!" But I'm grinning all over my face as I throw myself into my stroke like it's the final 50 meter interval!

But this is where the fun could start, as Eddie notes in his log:

'The tide is now pushing him hard back down towards Calais... Chris and I have had a little bet on where we will land. Looks like I won as we will land near to Cap Blanc-Nez.

Lots of people have sent regards. Deal Tri Club have passed on their best as well as Nicky at Dover Coastguard...'

Cap Blanc-Nez is closer to Calais and north of Cap Gris-Nez. As Tony explained, not the shortest line across as the weather hasn't pushed us in the direction we anticipated. However, I am now getting pushed up the Channel towards Calais, so if I weaken at this point or delay unnecessarily at the feeds we could drift and miss our intended landfall. No chance! My stroke rate is over 60 and you'd have to break my arms and cut my legs off to stop me at this point!

Feed 16, 6.30pm (The last stop)

"Good. Fucking get ready!" I'm chewing my way through a honey sandwich but my brain is all on THE END: I can't wait to get there!

"Yeah:, half an hour roughly," replies Ed.

I'm still eating and drinking like a good 'un. Hey - there's still a wee bike ride to do, right?

"You've picked up the pace nicely," notes Eddie, "it has been noted!"

"Anything to oblige." I eye him meaningfully over the feed bottle. "'I have been sitting on my arse for 2 days - what do you expect?!"

"There's a mile to the finish." Tony is leaning over at me, "and the other two pilot boats who were ahead of us - they were both relay teams - well, they haven't finished yet, so you may well beat them in!"

But I'm completely oblivious and am just staring at the coast just one mile away: FUCKING COME ON!!

"You hear that, Andy?" Ed can see I'm miles away, "You're a mile from the finish..."

The word 'finish' is the one which gets through and I turn round.

"No - what? Hey, I've got earplugs in, y'know!"

So Ed has to repeat it all. In my 'take-no-prisoners-let's-just-nail-this-sucker-once-and-for-all' mood I particularly like the bit about beating relay teams;

"Bloody poofs!"

"Well, they haven't been trained by us!" comes the reply from above me.

"Well, there is that, of course..." and I salute the man to whom I have bared at least some of my soul over the past 4 months. Hey, it's all worth it now.

One last look ahead "One mile - and then this office is closing!"

If you could have sat me down before all this and asked me to try and describe what this point would feel like, I wouldn't have even got close.

It felt like I was flying - I wasn't because my fast twitch muscle fibres has lost their 'fast' a long time ago - but I was certainly swimming the best I had all day. It was flat calm again and as my senses heightened I began lose my self in the absolute joy of the last few hundred yards of the biggest swim of my life.

With me on the boat were some of the people most dear to me in the whole world. I remember briefly that there was a time when Charly very definitely was not going to be with me for the crossing. I catch sight of her grinning like a loon on the deck and I say a quiet prayer of thanks that we had the courage of our convictions. It meant so much that she was here to share this...

Ed is stripping off to his trunks and I wonder briefly why until I realise he's getting ready to swim. 'Come on, then!' I just want to share this stuff and a few moments later I get my first swimming company of the day.

400 yards to go. Only one thing for it then: I up the pace and watch Ed's response to my left. He's swimming with head up to keep

and eye on me, the boat, and the rocks ahead. I see him up his stroke rate and I grin manically to myself: I've no idea what I'm doing - but it just feels bloody brilliant!

I'm breathing to my left and grinning my challenge to him with every breath. Head up for three strokes "I'm waiting for you to kick!" We're already swimming fast but Ed grins over in response and surges again and I concentrate on staying pinned to his hip. 20, 50, 100 yards: "Hell's bells!" Ed looks over at Tim and Charlotte between mouthfuls of water and is probably wondering just where the heck this lot came from! C'mon you bastard, drop your head - show me you're starting to hurt! Fat chance: Ed starts to pull away as what feels like a refrigerator jumps on my back, so in a last desperate show of bravado I throw in a few strokes of butterfly for good measure before rolling onto my back laughing and spluttering for all I'm worth.

Ooooh, that was fun!

Ed and I swim easily in for the last few yards. I'm very peacefully slipping through the water as the sun dips below the horizon to my right. Well, bugger me: we're going to do it. After the tears this morning and the fears for the weather, we really are going to do it. Get sorted, some food, rest, then let's get on the bike and finish this fucker...

Touch. I realise now why Eddie has come with me - and it wasn't for the impromptu sprint session! It's very rocky underfoot and I can't stand up on my own. This really throws me as I've never had this problem with any of the big training swims, but he knows what he's doing and levers me upright.

"Fucking awesome, mate - fucking awesome!" A huge bearhug and a massive grinning match before I turn and face the boat bobbing about 100 yards away. I throw my arms aloft and scream at the top of my voice: "CHARLEEEEE!!!"

We have a few brief moments before climbing into the dingy which has followed us in. I've been on stuff which is definitely performance-enhancing for at least the last hour, but now I really am walking on water. We don't say much - and I'm probably incapable of coherence anyway - as Ed has been where I am and it is very, very special.

Tony heads us back to the boat, and I'm impressed that I'm

almost able to climb aboard unaided. I'm still wearing a grin as wide as my face. Chris greets me with a handshake and tries to out-grin me: no chance! "Well done, mate!" I'm laughing again as I catch sight of Charly almost bouncing up and down behind Chris in her excitement:

"Channel Swimming Husband!" She gets a big, soggy wetsuit hug and saltwater kiss for her trouble - then has to steady us both as the boat rocks. We just hold each other laughing uncontrollably. I point over her shoulder to the shore: "It's just a load of rocks! Just a big fucking cliff..! That's all it is..!?!"

"Yep - that's right!" Tim is still filming it all. I look straight at him.

"Put down that camera and give me a hug, you bastard!"

From Eddie's Log:
'Swim time 12 hours 38 minutes.
Approx 100m east of Dover Patrol Memorial on Cap Blanc-Nez on a little sand beach between rocks. Andy was absolutely delighted - he laughed with sheer joy.

We returned quickly to the waiting boat with Tony. Andy dressed and looked in good condition. Off we went to Calais.

I swam the last half mile with Andy - he had the cheek to want to race! He picked his stroke rate up and made good headway. He even had the nerve to do a couple of fly strokes.

Everyone on the boat is over the moon. We nearly did not start as the forecast looked crap. I really thought it would blow up. Andy was strong this morning and decided today or never: I am glad he did.'

Reflections from Charlotte
We'd just not thought about what would happen at the end. Tony was getting the dingy ready and Ed just disappeared - then reappeared in his wetsuit! I just looked at him and said 'Are you swimming then?' And he said something about having to get you out once you reached the shore...

We were teasing him about going in - it wasn't difficult as it was obvious he was dying to get in and join you! - then he just dived in and swam up to you. Then he swam you away from the boat a bit - and Tim and I are still trying to film, and you're just disappearing!

We were all very excited by now, the shore looked so close but it was still over half a mile away. And then you started racing - which was great! It was such a rush to see you swimming so well, having fun, just enjoying it!

As you both swam in to shore we could see some people on the cliffs who were waving, but they seemed so tiny. We could hardly see you either, so couldn't film you emerging from the sea. I didn't hear you shouting - just the sea gulls complaining about being disturbed just as they'd all settled on the cliffs for the night.

I was really impressed to see you get out of the dingy and back into the boat on your own, I'd not been with you at the end of a long swim before, but you looked in good nick, though very cold and wet - surprise surprise! So I had this big cold clammy wet seal thing to kiss, but was very pleased to have you back!

Then of course it was bedlam as we all rushed around again trying to find your bag and making sure we had everything to hand which we hadn't as we were all far too excited! I got a towel over you and stuff but... Tim and I were just really excited and bowled over by it all, it was like, whoa - we're not worthy!

It seemed to go dark really quickly once we were all back on the boat. My main concern was keeping you warm. Lots of cups of tea, but not much food at this point as we'd eaten it all, but it was getting colder very quickly by now so we were all just piling the clothes on.

As we neared Calais there was much discussion between Chris and Eddie where Eddie Clarke would be and what we would have to do as we came into harbour. In the end Chris just cleared us on the radio - and then there was Eddie Clarke - exactly where he said he would be!

You seemed remarkably healthy again and I was shattered! I just had that 'big fresh air exhausting day feeling' again...

This is supposed to mean 12 hours! We're in Calais and I'm still on a high after the swim. Now where's that restaurant?

Cycling

"The wind always blows hardest at the top of the mountain"

Ginny Leng, Three Day Eventing

Sunday, 21st September

A 4.30am alarm (French time) rouses us all from a rough night. We've all slept fitfully due to a combination of outside noise - we're just in a car park in the middle of the harbour complex - and the challenge of getting all 5 of us horizontal in the motorhome! At least Charly and I have had the double bunk...

At 5.30am I'm on the road and away. The last leg, let's just get this thing done! Even at this time of the morning it is warm: I've started with my arm warmers on, but very quickly go down to short sleeves and shorts. With the headlights of the following motor home lighting my way, we quickly clear Calais and I settle down in a 52/15 gearing and a good 85-90 rpm. It all feels good and the bike has that lovely smooth almost purring sound, so I enjoy 'dark and no street lights' riding as we head through the countryside as the skies slowly lighten on our way to the first marker, which is Boulogne.

Reflections from Charlotte

We saw you off then I just fell asleep again - I was just shattered! It was dark so The Two Eddies took turns to drive and Tim and I slept: 2 hours, but it set me up for the rest of the day...

Sunday in France is also the day, just like in the UK, when the cyclists come out to play. So it wasn't long before I was encountering kindred spirits on two wheels. Cyclists are higher up the food chain in France than in good ole Blighty, and my occasional triathlon racing on this side of the Channel had taught me that 'Cycling Is Sacred' over here. What it also appeared to mean as far as French triathletes were concerned was that the strategy of 'swim OK, ride like the wind, run like erm, something a lot slower' was just fine. So as I hook up with my new temporary chums, we're all doing the 'I'm really not trying very hard or trying to race you' bit. Boys, eh?

This was the first test - of my language skills. How do you credibly explain at about 7 o'clock in the morning to a couple of unsuspecting locals that you've come via 'La Manche a nager' and before that 'depart a Londres a pied pour Dover..... enroute to un triathlon tres grande'? Well, I did try, but I may have stretched the common currency of the bike a little bit too far. Still, a great excuse to improvise with much gesturing and guttural nasal noises. I think my riding companions got the gist - but whether they believed it all is entirely another matter! Ah, le Roast Beef!

The sun is hot already as I clear Boulogne and head for the first stop at 50 miles. I'd broken the ride up very simply: stops at 50, 100 and 150 miles. This would also be a change for the crew; contact would be much less than the previous 2 legs, which meant that they would be less able to read me as I was hidden behind cycling helmet and shades. The motor home was leap-frogging me periodically as Eddie Clarke had to choose his stopping points with care. So the guys would go on ahead and stop and heckle me as I went past, or drive slowly ahead of me, keeping in sight if navigation was tricky through a town, for example. If we met at junction or traffic lights then Charly would take the opportunity to refresh my bottles and have a snatched conversation. My plan though, was to keep moving between the 50 mile points.

8.00 am and it's already warm...

But, by about 40 miles I'm starting to fade. This catches me by surprise at first - tired so soon? - But it's not long before I realise I've ridden this first section way too hard. It's not been flat at all, and although the road surface is orders of magnitude above what I'm used to, the hills have been rolling and just unrelenting. Without hedgerows there is no shade at all and even this early in the morning I am starting to cook a little more than I would like...

Above all I'm paying for my enthusiastic start to the ride and a mindset of 'this thing's pretty much in the bag!' The previous day's efforts may just be having something to do with it as well...

Bollocks. Over the next few miles I successfully get myself into a lovely downward spiral, feeling more and more pissed off as I am forced to select smaller and smaller gears to keep the bike moving. Seeing the motor home stopped ahead of me is a relief as I take it for the 50 mile stop. Not so, I'm only at 40 miles and have to get going again.

I am now more than a mite pissed off with Life, The Universe And Everything and to make matters even more interesting, I am starting to go light-headed as the energy levels drop through the floor. I can't believe I'm feeling like this so soon. Jesus! I've got over 100 miles still to do, for fuck's sake! OK - don't panic, just get to 50, stop, eat, chill - you'll be fine, just get some food in your then we'll see.........

After a little over two and three quarter hours on the road I wobble into the 50 mile lay-by. It's monosyllable communication time again, and I stay in my cave while I shovel down a pan full of macaroni cheese and a plate full of sandwiches.

Reflections from Charlotte
You looked a bit grumpy at 45 miles, so I figured you might be getting hungry - it's usually the case!

............And by 50 miles I could definitely see that you were not a happy boy! It was fairly clear when you arrived that you were not going to be very communicative - so I let you get on with it and trusted the food to work it's magic. I could see that it hadn't been very nice out there - so open and exposed on the roads. But hey - you felt better after food!

I certainly did, and suddenly the world did not look such a bad place. A little on the hot side admittedly, but I WAS smiling again! Chatting again with Ed I knew now that I'd overcooked it and so made a decision to ride more with my head than my heart for the next section. OK, lesson learned, this thing is not quite in the bag, and it now has my respect once again. Can I try that again, please?

Onwards after a half-hour break as the sun climbs and the day heats up once again. I'm down to a vest and drinking once again like a good'un. My cadence is down to 80 rpm and I'm definitely spending more time in the small chain ring. It doesn't matter, just keep the pedals turning, control the effort, and use the gears. If that means the granny gear on the climbs, then granny gear it is - just keep the cadence up and the effort even. Move around on the descents, flex the back and shake the shoulders out. Just keep doing what you're doing. You're up on the pace and through the worst bit - so just stay with this!

Reflections from Charlotte

The crew were dissenting a bit at this point as there was a serious requirement for coffee and croissants! We were low on food - and I knew I had to feed you - so we were just eating anything amidst intense bouts of navigating.

The roads were just soooo long and exposed. There was nowhere to stop and we couldn't cruise with you so we just had to leave you for long periods and go on ahead to find somewhere to pull over. It must have been boring for you!

It was very hard to get a feel for how you were because we just couldn't see you. It was pretty frustrating for me - I wasn't driving so all I could do was to line up the food for the next feed. I got quite proficient at wedging the pan and myself on our little gas cooker and asking for warning when corners were imminent - all highly illegal, but it helped us to look after you!

There's that bloke again on the roadside - I'm sure I've seen him before! How the heck did he get in front of me? I briefly question my sanity, but as I figure I'm not quite in pink elephant territory yet, I consign the observation to the 'irrelevant' file. But a few miles further on, there he is again!

Charlotte
Oh, the hitch hiker! Now that WAS funny! We thought we'd really piss you off with this because we picked him up after you went past him. We took him ahead of you, you passed him - and then we picked him up again! We laughed our socks off 'cos we thought it'd just do your head in!

Ah, the playground is truly a cruel place.... But I was doing OK, just getting my head down and getting on with it. The wind was getting up now - but it was a warm wind and it was in my face - and as we were going in a straight line, I knew that this was going to be the pattern for the rest of the day. I remember that Eddie had a tailwind on his ride... and then I also remember that the same wind was the one which gave him a serious kicking in the Channel. With one hand the Lord giveth...

The lure of the 100 mile stop is strong though. I've put a lasso around it miles ago and with every pedal revolution I'm pulling myself in. More than half way. Just get there, you know you recharge well, so just get there and get ready for the next bit...

This second 50 mile section takes me about a quarter of an hour longer than the first, and despite starting to feel decidedly cooked - and a little uncomfortable in the undercarriage, (!) I've managed the effort much better this time. A little after 1 pm I climb gratefully into the shade of the motor home and lie down as Charlotte covers me with a wet towel from the fridge.

Reflections from Charlotte
I knew you were weary, but heck, you were going to be! My big concern was that you kept it together because of the traffic.

One tray full of food and about 30 minutes later I push off once again, turn the corner, and am confronted by the sight of the biggest *@£&* hill so far! Hey - great stopping place guys!?! But it's more resignation than anything else and I have a wry smile, click into my smallest gear and crawl my way upwards on a full stomach. Lovely!

Charlotte
....Then, there was the big hill immediately after the 100 mile stop. At about half way up we looked at each other sheepishly and Ed said that if he'd have remembered it was there he'd have stopped after it! We'd all perked up after coffee and croissants again at 100 miles but this really chastened us for a bit...!

It's hot open and exposed with a headwind thrown in all the way to Paris.

Coming up to about 120 miles I pass the motor home pulled over. It looks like the guys are stopping to get supplies. I hear a vague shout of 'straight on' as I wordlessly pedal past. It's very hot and my world is once again shrinking down to the essentials. I've been climbing off and on for a while as the sun continues to beat down and the wind picks up. Cresting this latest section I'm exposed on what looks like a wide plateau with absolutely no shade. Traffic is sporadic and the road just stretches out ahead. The mind games begin as I begin to wilt. I'm expecting the crew to come past at any time but as the minutes go by without this happening I being to question whether I am on the right road. Did I miss a turning? They did say 'straight on' didn't they? So where the hell are they then?! And this bloody wind! I'm out of the saddle pedalling downhill, for chrissake! No, you're OK, just keep pedalling... Fuck that! It's bastard hot, I'm tired - so where the fuck are they?!

But looking around behind me reveals no motor home so as the last remnants of rational thought leave me, I jerk the bike to a halt and climb off and just sit down on the road side with no thought to where I am or what this will mean for the guys. I've had enough of the draining heat, the effort and the isolation and just want to stop NOW: So fuck it - fuck it all....

Almost immediately the motor home pulls up. The door opens and I push my way in as Charly and Tim look at me in alarm. "I'm cooking out here - I just need to get out of this heat for a while!" I figure that's explanation enough for everybody as I simply lie down on the floor of the vehicle, prop my feet up and close my eyes. But I'd picked a really bad place to throw my toys out...

Reflections from Charlotte

We'd stopped again for supplies which is why we were behind you... But you'd stopped in a really bad place, which was why Eddie was looking for some shade for you. You were only a mile out from the next village, which was what we were aiming for anyway. As we pulled up Ed said 'we're not stopping.' You had a paddie - so we stopped - and promptly got moved on by some gendarmes who came to see what we were doing! They were not happy - we'd stopped on a really fast road - so Ed was angry because you'd made a bad call and almost endangered the whole crew and the event itself... I kept out of the way as I could see what was happening: it was going to be 'Clash of the

Titans' between the two of you! But to be fair you pulled back from that, and we were 'right, no drama - let's just move and get sorted then...'

But it was a close one. I could see that Ed genuinely couldn't see what all the fuss was about as his mindset was, 'you have a problem? Just find somewhere to stop, cool down, have something to eat - have a sleep if you want - we've got plenty of time....' That's how he did his - but it was not how I was doing mine.

In my mind I was in a race so I was still pushing at this point. OK, it was slow and painful, but I wanted to put the best time I could on this bike leg and THAT meant there was no place for 3 course meals and afternoon naps by the roadside. That may work for you Ed, but this is MY show and I'll do it how I want to do it!

As I lay there with my eyes closed, my chest heaving and the blood pounding through my head, part of my mind raged silently; don't you understand - I'm in a FUCKING RACE here! You're supposed to be MY SUPPORT - so where the bloody hell were you when I needed you!?!' Fortunately, the other part of my head was being a little more helpful. 'Shut up - don't say a word, it's not important. You've fucked up, so just build the bridge, get your shit together and get on with it. These folks are your friends, remember....?'

Performance is emotional - and if it matters, it will hurt to fall short...

Oh yeah, I remember now...

It was as close as we ever got to cross words during the whole summer. Pretty good when you consider I have an ego the size of a planet and we're all pretty driven folks!

So I got my proverbial shit together with the help of cold towels, food, drink, shade and some TLC from folks who mattered. Remember what you're doing and why, huh?

Reflections from Charlotte
Ed doesn't get annoyed, but on this occasion he genuinely was as

he thought you'd made a stupid move: you just stopped in the heat with no shade - so you're just getting hotter. It was a bad place to stop the van and we couldn't help you there. So I could see why he was angry - and he was kinda justified... But being 'irrational' is so unusual for you! Certainly up to that point you'd been pretty smart about everything you'd done, so it was like 'Whoa! Where did THIS come from?' You were a victim of your own success in that respect - but we all knew you'd feel better after food and a cool down, as that had been the pattern all along.

I could see that Ed was genuinely rattled by the Gendarmes, and no wonder! It would have been disastrous if they'd stopped us and made us explain our situation or have to go off with them to a station - the implications for the Challenge were huge: so definitely six of one and half a dozen of the other between the two of you!

It was the only time when there were any fireworks - and whilst it was faintly alarming it wasn't that surprising - you're pushing, right? I also know you are Mr. Grumpy when you're hungry, so I knew what it would take to fix it and that you'd be OK and on your way again. But it was definitely a bit awkward for everyone for a moment or two!

Toys and prams not withstanding (!) the next 20 miles or so were the hardest of the lot. I was tired in every sense now and hurting most places as well. It felt like I was crawling along in places and simply moving from one landmark to the next. I'd pick a point in the distance and fix on it, then another, then another. Or I'd count the pedal revolutions with my gaze fixed to the tarmac about 3 metres in front of me.

Reflections from Charlotte

I knew you were not exactly a happy bunny so I did make an effort to lie in the back of the motor home by the window as we went through towns and pull faces as you! I didn't know whether you noticed - with your helmet and shades on it was very difficult to tell - but I could see some reaction when we pulled alongside you at junctions...

The cycle leg was easy feed-wise: 50, 100, 150 miles. Macaroni cheese, rice pudding and super noodles. But coming up to 150 miles

I was starting to think 'help - what have I got left?' I thought you'd be pretty pissed off with all the carbohydrates by now; you'd had very little protein so I thought I'd add a tin of tuna as well. I do wonder whether we should have made more of a fuss over the food stops as they were key because they were the only real time we got to interact with you: you know - little white tablecloth, silver service, 3 courses, that sort of thing (!) - it might have made more of a difference...

Difference or not, the tuna pasta at 150 miles was not only nectar to my taste buds but woke the rest of me up as well. I grovelled into the stop, but it was a different story going back out again! This was just as well as we were now starting to hit the wider faster roads as we neared Paris, and I could see the crew was worried that in my tired state the risks of faster heavier traffic would be magnified. Perversely, the last miles of the Challenge would be when I would need my cycling wits and my energy the most.

We needn't have worried. Whether it was the 'speed up or die' realisation - self-preservation IS a powerful motivator! - or Charly's magic feed, I sped on to the dual carriage ways on the big chain ring pushing bigger gears with a good cadence once again. The trick was to watch the slip roads coming onto the carriage way from my right, and just pray I wouldn't get hit from behind as I crossed slip roads leaving the carriage way! Move your ass Mounce! Speed is your friend here!

Then the first real setback. We make a turn at a big junction and very quickly find ourselves lost. We pull over and the guys spent a few fraught minutes trying to figure out whilst I prop myself up against the bike, drink and calmly wait it out. The decision is made to backtrack and try again, so rather than getting me to re-trace my steps, Ed chucks me and the bike in the back and I stretch out on a bunk and close my eyes while the motor home returns the way we have just come.

Reflections from Charlotte
I was worried you'd fall asleep - and desperate that you didn't - but I could also tell you were in 'OK, I'm just not going to flap about this

till it's sorted' mode: so don't hassle me - just sort it out!

I felt like I shouldn't get involved in the map reading at first as it wasn't my job - so I resisted for as long as I could bear it! But I could tell Ed was struggling. He'd been let down at short notice by his first choice driver/navigator for this leg - and of course he'd never seen this bit from a van before! We really missed the other guy here - so I got involved! It helped us both, but although we had good maps it's amazing how used to OS maps you get!

It was a relief to see that you got into the outskirts OK, and you seemed quite perky. I knew you could ride in heavy traffic, but I also knew how tired I was - so God knows what you were like - and it wasn't as though we saw any other cyclists any more!

But, you knew you were in Paris and nearly there, but it was sooo frustrating for us not being able to take you straight in as we then got stuck in traffic!

It turns out that EVERYONE goes into Paris on a Sunday evening and the roads were crammed with traffic backing up from every junction. The picture I'd painted in my mind about hurtling through Paris and up the Champs Elysées on these last few miles quickly evaporated. It was clear it was going to be stop-start all the way in! There was absolutely nothing I could do except wait in the traffic for the van, so I sat up, enjoyed the sights and sounds and started to smile as the dusk settled. Almost there....

Reflections from Charlotte

We were definitely more in a flap than you at this point, which was a shame, as we didn't really get to enjoy it. We did try - but we were desperate to make sure you were on the right track. The thought of taking you any further than you needed to go at this point was just awful! That's what I was worried about - I just wanted you to stop: just let it all be finished!

And then we started to hit the one way system, and that was just a bitch! We were using our torches to read the map now because it was so bloody dark in the van!

I was pleased that you seemed happy at this point. Eddie Clarke was very good - he was so patient with us - though even he started to fray around the edges on a couple of occasions so we decided to stop and ask for directions. We knew we were close as the avenues were getting bigger and it was definitely getting very swish!

And then we turned a corner, and it was like, 'Oh my God - there it is!'

And there it was: The Arc in all it's floodlit glory just 100 yards away at the top of the avenue. Eddie Clarke toots madly on the horn behind me as I turn in the saddle. "Go on Andy - go on!" There's frantic waving so I ride slowly away as it all starts to feel a little surreal. I'm jolted back to reality though by the free-for-all chaos which is the Place de la Concorde. How the hell do I get across this?! But almost by magic, as I nose my front wheel into the outlying lanes of traffic five to six cars deep, the cars all slow and allow me to ride across....do they know what I've done to get here?

I'm still smiling to myself in wonder as I dismount and wheel the bike the last few yards to the stonework. Surrounded by scaffolding it's not looking it's best, but that's not really an issue right now! A gendarme intercepts me; something about not bringing my bike into this inner area? I try and explain that I might have a really good case for doing just this, (!) but even the very short version of the nearly 300 miles of self-propelled effort fail to move him, so I do my best Gallic shrug and prop the bike up: no way are you gonna bust my bubble now, sunshine!

With a thump something cannons into me - and Charly wraps her arms around my neck with tears streaming down her cheeks after a flat out sprint to catch up with me! It's a long, "just hold me tight babe" husband and wife moment as we laugh, smile and have a little cry - but most of us all just stare up at the Arc towering above us. Well. We're really here then..........

As the rest of the guys arrive it's a mixture of mutual congratulations, relief and a few group hugs before Ed suddenly stops: "Andy - did you stop the clock?" I pause, and then think better of messing with him just this once - so just grin and pull out the stopwatch. 14 hours 17 minutes in the saddle. Ed just looks at me and lets out a long breath:

'Well, thank fuck for that!'

Charlotte

I was just bloody grateful to Eddie Clarke at this point as he was the one who marshalled us. I'd not thought about what would happen at all here, and he said, 'Right - I'm stopping right now!' Because he knew he wouldn't be able to get the motor home any closer. I'm thinking, 'OK - but shit, it's still miles away!' So we're all rushing around and I grab my bag and camera and run like a nutter up the street - jumping over tramps and everything! I then spend ages trying to get across the Place de la Concorde before remembering that there had to be a subway somewhere! I could hear Tim thumping along behind me and I was thinking, 'C'mon Tim, you can do it!'

I was so excited and just wanted to get to you to see that you were still alive and had finished - I was definitely a little more emotional than you! I was soooo relieved - just enormously relieved that you were there! Yes, I was excited and pleased - and I guess if you'd got the World Record I'd have been more excited - but it was definitely more a feeling of relief.

Wasn't it great that the Arc was covered in scaffolding for us?!!

And you seemed fine! Absolutely fine - not knackered at all - just quietly pleased, like: 'Good. Yes. Fantastic. Result. Job done!'

Job done indeed: Nearly 300 miles and 115 hours: No World Record, but a successful crossing for only the second time, new fastest times for each stage - and every damn bit of it so very, very special.

Now anyone for a very large pizza?!

TEAM ME

Get the apologies in first! If I've missed anyone then this next line is for you: THANK YOU! Boy, was it all a bit special - and you all helped make it so.

Bring those closest to you with you on the journey from the start.
Could I have done this without Charly? Well, we'll never know - but one thing I do know is that the scary bits were less scary and the sweet bits tasted even sweeter because of her. Hey, my wife rocks! Charly, just read the front bit, you'll get the idea...

Eddie Ette: you started all this! It takes Big Ones to pioneer anything, and my friend, you have them! It was a privilege to follow for a while. For the belief, the bullying, the stories, the piss-taking, the tea and toast, the ocean-time, the fish, the secrets, your home, and the damned hard work - thanks for it all, man.

To our families, who probably went through all sorts of stuff! My Mum for her unwavering enthusiasm, (once she got over the initial shock - and hey, that phone call at the Arc d'Triomphe made us all smile!) and my Dad for reminding me just how big a deal this was. Thanks Dad - we tried to be careful! All my grandparents: sorry - it was just something we had to do! Simon for doing vintage brother stuff, and Sue and Denis for letting me rope their youngest daughter in on it all. Five years of courtship and 2 of marriage have given them some time to get used to this latest addition to the family - but it was still a hell of a stretch: thanks for stretching with us and letting us reflect and recuperate at Bank House!

To Anne for being Big Sister Sensible and Stewart for one of the best emails 'just keep going, you crazy fool!' messages I ever got. Stephen, Diane, Anna, Sarah and Helena for bananas, and Tim, Max and Jess for serious reality checks. More for you, Tim, later...

My (Other) Crew

Eddie Clarke for just being absolutely unflappable and feeding me sweets during those last nerve-racking miles into Paris. Tim for being Tim, wrestling with cameras, doing enthusiastic even when half dead with fatigue, fielding families, and getting this damn thing on film for us! John Williams for the Healing Hands - we've come a long way from the Premier classroom, huh? Chris and Tony in Seafarer for taming the Channel for me and sharing an incredible twelve and a half hours.

The Portland Chapter

Lynne Ette for being a rock - and doing caring like you wouldn't believe. Tom Watch for timeless and priceless knowledge, hours on the boat - and Sheila, for letting him out! Wendy for some kindred spirit stuff and for keeping me humble those first few weeks. Kate for those priceless photos. Ron for keeping me safe during a watershed Round Portland swim and Paul shepherding in a gibbering wreck during the last part of Weymouth-Lulworth. Marci for the talc at the beach hut for that second swim of the day back in those early weeks. Gren and family for the sanctuary - and More Good Advice! Paul and his cigars at Lulworth. And Steve Gershon, you get a mention here because it all started on a bike in the Dorset hills: training just dilutes the race experience, man!

City of Coventry Swimming Club

Adam for the Definition and the Apples, Mick and Rachel for lifting me at 6 hours in the Channel, Nick for putting out the word when we got back, (What did you do last weekend?!) Grace, Sophie and Helen for all the 'Go Coach' stuff!

Those Who Helped with our Shopping List

- John and Lynne at Hole In The Wall, Hinckley for the polo shirts.
- Tina McEwen and Denise Holzer at Business Link Leicestershire for the mailshot.

- Graham and Terry at Hinckley and South Wigston Cycles for 187 miles of working bicycle.
- Nikki and Tim at Dragons for seriously functional and very cool eyewear - and Nik for the texting frenzy!
- Biddie Foord at Terrapin for the wetsuit and emergency repairs!
- Nigel and Sue Swift at Tri Bike for bottles, tubes and stuff.
- Amanda Newton and the team at Brownhills Leisure Group, Newark for coming to our rescue at the last minute with a motor home to die for!
- Stephanie Sammut at Soreen for a supply of my fave malt loafs and chewy bars.
- Mike Vaughan Cycles for the bike lights.
- Dave Hillman and his massage couch for keeping my body together during the training.

Just Rootin' For Ya, High Fives From Paris, and More Help With The Shopping

Paul and Brenda at the French connection. Matthew Mitchell, Richard & Mhairi Billington, Margaret Townson.

Hinckley Running Club - especially: Adrian Whalley, Richard and Linda Whitelegg, Louise Oliver, Kim Lewis, Kate Whetton, Dave and Penny Masser, Jenni and Keith - sorry about the wedding..! Oh yeah - and The Hairy Hippy Household for some decidedly dodgy dreams!

John and Norah Whittaker. Tim and Cath Puffer - yep, that £5 was bloody well spent! Bridget and Jack and Jane and Stephen for the last 3 years. Tall Bloke for Focus-Balance-Discovery, Mark Kleanthous for being even more insane, Julie Robinson for a Blast From The Past, Geraud Mousnier for a surprise bon voyage, Dr. Martin Yelling, Leyshon and Ray for being on the M42, Howard Vine, Bill and Vanessa, Janet Hudson, Malcolm and Rhona, James MacWilliam, Vivienne Kingdom, Steve 'Moments' Bailey, John and Nicola Lunt,

Philipa in Oz.

Gemma, Smooth Booth, Bert and Helen for agonising through it all with us, Chris Flavell, Steve Trew for lighting the blue touch paper for us in the triathlon world. Mike Ireland, Chris and Sandra, Best Bloke & Best Bird, Gill, Georgie and Co. and French Bird.

Angela Hawkins - and look what it led to! - Michael Godden at PPD, all the folks at Be Clear Ltd: Christine, Jane, Claire, Mike - and his good lady Jo. Alice Talo, Simon Bozeat for the Big Shout en route! Patti Bailey & Ian Warner at MICE.

Mark Salmon, Lawrence Littler, Vince Mayne, Paul Groves and all at Deal Tri and Nicky at Dover Coastguard. Maria at the Longfield Guest House, Dover for bed, breakfast and ice many times over!

David Shephard of The Performance Partnership, London: Thanks for the head stuff and the breakfast! Charles & Laurice: thanks for the intro to this man - and so much more besides over the last 3 years!

John Barwick at Coutts & Co Ltd, London.

Pauline Kearney and Adrian Lole at the Royal Life Saving Society for banging the drum for us!

Our Friends In Media-Land
Rosie Harding, Carolyn & Sara at BBC TV< Nottingham
BBC Radio Kent
John Barber & Martin Ballard at BBC Radio Leicester
Ellie at the Tamworth Herald
Zoe at the Rugby Advertiser
Mark at the Hinckley Times
Julian Crabtree at Sky TV: over to you!
Folkestone Radio
Radio KMFM

The Dover Express

Chris Day & Andrew at Chris Day Creative Services & Filament Publishing for believing in us enough to help us put this book (and other goodies) together. That was pretty good intro, Vicki!

Manorfield Primary School, Stony Stanton
Steve The Head and Gill The Teach, Kids: Emma, Samuel, Emma, Matthew, Christian, David, Katie, Akhia, Lucy, Joshua, Jacob, Kai, Ryan, Oliver, Rhys, Rheanna, Victoria, Peter, Matthew, Cameron, Hayden, Sam and Arnie-George.

Above: *Feed time in the Channel - don't touch the boat!*

Above: *Eddie checks progress in the Channel*

Left: *It was a long day for the crew as well. Charly keeps watch.*

Below: *the forecast was wrong and the weather blessed us all day.*

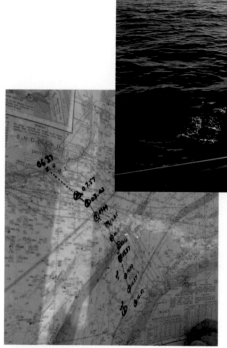

Above: *The sun sparkles on the wavetops as we near the French coast.*

Left: *Keeping track of the swim.*

Below: *Sunset in the last half mile and Eddie has joined me.*

Left: *With Eddie about to start the last leg.*

Below: *The roads were long and open. Even at 8.00am it's warm.*

Above:
The 50m stop and my sense of humour has returned! Post food with Tim.

Left:
Pushing on towards 100m.

Below:
100m and I'm enjoying the shade.

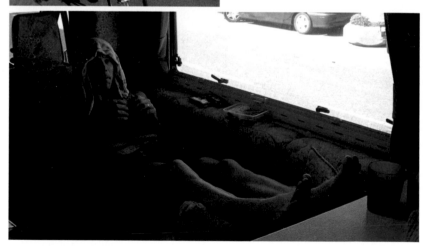

Above: *Feeling insignificant yet?*

Below Left: *"Just tell me where to ride!" Closing my eyes for a few minutes as the crew retrace our route after getting lost in the outskirts of Paris*

Below:
The last few miles in Paris were the toughest for the crew. Charly and Eddie Clarke try and figure out the one way system

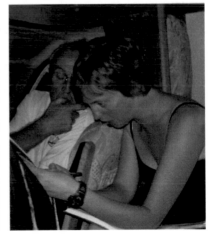

Left:
We're really here! A husband and wife moment at the Arc de Triomphe

Below:
Shattered but delighted: we did it! (From left to right) Eddie Ette, Tim Jury, Me, Charly and Eddie Clarke.

Appendices

ENDUROMAN Arch to Arc Challenge: Comparative Times.

	Andy Mouncey	Eddie Ette (World Record)
RUN START	0040 Sept 17 '03	0115 Jul 30 '01
RUN FINISH	19.10	21.49
RUN SPLIT	18 hrs 30 min	20 hrs 34 min
WAITING	59 hrs 47 min	19 hrs 35 min
SWIM START	0637 Sat Sept 20 '03	1724 Jul 31 '01
SWIM FINISH	1915	1054 Aug 1 '01
SWIM SPLIT	12 hrs 38 min	17 hrs 30 min
WAITING	10 hrs 16 min	4 hrs 38 min
CYCLE START	0531 Sun Sept 21 '03	1532 Aug 1 '01
CYCLE FINISH	1948	1020 Aug 2 '01
CYCLE SPLIT	14 hrs 17 min	18 hrs 48 min
TOTAL ELAPSED TIME	115 hrs 08 min	80 hrs 5 min

Training Summary May - Sept 2003

Week No	1		2		3		4		5	
Swim	5.5	5	6	6	10.5	7	4.5	4	7.5	5
Bike	2	1	3.5	3	4	2	1.5	2	3.75	3
Run	2.5	3	6	5	2	3	4	3	2.75	2
Weights	0	0	0.5	1	0	0	0.75	1	1	2
Total	10	9	16	15	16.5	12	10.5	10	15	12

Week No	6		7		8		9		10	
Swim	8.5	5	4.5	1	8	4	6.5	2	4.5	4
Bike	1.75	1	2.5	2	6	3	2.5	1	3	2
Run	4	4	5	3	8	4	10	5	8.5	5
Weights	0.75	2	0.75	1	0.75	1	0	0	0.5	1
Total	15	12	13	7	22	12	19	8	16.5	12

Week No	11		12		13		14		15		16	
Swim	10.5	4	5	3	2	3	12.75	3	3.5	3	6.5	5
Bike	3.75	2	2.25	1	1.5	2	4.75	3	3.5	2	3.5	2
Run	6.75	4	6	2	5.5	3	8.25	3	3.5	2	3.5	3
Weights	0.5	1	0.75	1	0.5	1	0.5	1	0	0	0	0
Total	22.5	11	14.5	7	9.5	8	27.25	10	10	7	13.5	10

Key

	No. of Training Hours per week in italics on grey
	No. of Training Sessions per week in normal type on white

The key for the whole thing was to be healthy and strong - in that order. That meant controlling diet, rest, stress - and weight training. My triathlon history goes back to 1987, and I'd trained and raced every year since then. The result was I'd got an awful lot in the bank, which meant I could springboard to 'Arch Condition' in 3-4 months. So my training took 16 years or 3-4 months depending how you want to measure it!

Specifically, the priority was the swim, so I invested most heavily in that. Next came the run, with the bike as the least most important part. The longest I ever rode in one session was 3 hours: this was mostly strength work, which I supplemented with weights. The longest I ran was 4 hours, and I did this twice. The balance between training and breakdown was a delicate one, and I built to blocks of back to back training sessions broken by blocks of no training or recovery sessions. My longest back to back session was 7 hours of continuous run-swim-cycle during week 12. Once the big swims started I switched to individual medley swimming for my pool sessions- i.e. the non-frontcrawl strokes. Weekly massage which alternated between upper and lower body was a vital preventative maintenance for the soft tissues.

The vast majority of the training was done on my own - deliberately. This was absolutely the case for all the key sessions which were also done around the middle of the day where I could fit them around work commitments. I continued to work through June and July, with August and September almost exclusively geared toward getting ready for the Challenge. I had no injuries though I was getting some tell-tale signs in my quad muscles in the last two weeks or so. Although I had favoured roads as the main surface I ran on, the unrelenting pounding did eventually prove my undoing at the 72 mile point. I was, however, as prepared as I could have been - though with hindsight perhaps it might have been more prudent to schedule in periods of walking for the first stage. However my goal was to RUN - so that was hardly on the agenda!

Big Swim Progressions

Week	Date	Swim Duration (hrs)	Notes
1	May 24	1	
	May 25	2	
	May 26	1	
3	Jun 6	2	
	Jun 7	2 (am) + 2 (pm)	
	Jun 8	2	
5	Jun 16	3.75	
6	Jun 27	2	
	Jun 28	5.25	
7	Jul 6	4.5	Weymouth to Lulworth 10 mile swim
8	Jul 10	6.25	
9	Jul 17	6	
11	Jul 31	8	
12	Aug 10	3	Round Portland 8 mile swim
14	Aug 22	10	

It took 14 weeks to build up to 10 hours – with the first 7 weeks definitely the hardest!

All my swims were done in the sea off Weymouth and Portland which meant an 8 hour round trip in the car each time – but that was the commitment I made. When you live in Leicestershire, decent sea swimming opportunities are a little thin on the ground...

Prior to this may longest swims had been ironman triathlon distance, (2.4 miles) and the 8 miles at Eddie's Chesil Challenge in September 2002 – and that had damned near killed me.

Swim Feeds (with notes from Eddie's log)

Feed	Time	Details	Duration
	0637	START	mins & secs
1	0720	1 bottle carb	1m 20s
2	0800	1 bottle carb / 2 chunks malt loaf / very happy!	2m
3	0845	1 bottle carb / 1 chunk banana	2m
4	0930	1 bottle carb / 1 chunk energy bar / smiles	1m 15s
5	1015	1 bottle carb / 1 chunk banana	1m 10s
6	1100	1 bottle carb / cup fruit chunks / malt loaf / chatty and asked how good is progress	3m
7	1146	1 bottle carb / 1 x chunk banana / 1 x chunk energy bar / winked to Charlotte – looks good!	2m 30s
8	1230	1/2 mug tea / 2 x Jaffa cake / 1 chunk malt loaf / 1 bottle carb / asked if he had broken the back of the swim – I was quick to say 1/2 way and no more: he needs to know lots to do yet…	3m 30s
9	1315	1 bottle carb / 2 x painkillers / 2 chunks malt loaf / says hip hurting	6m
10	1400	Cup of tea / 1/2 cup fruit chunks / jelly babies / asked for company, move to sunny side of the boat, swim closer	2m 30s
11	1445	1 bottle carb / 2 Jaffa cake / jelly babies / chatty again	2m
12	1530	Cup of tea / 2 x painkillers / chunk malt loaf	1m 30s
13	1615	1 bottle carb / malt loaf chunk / chunk banana / chatty – told no more than 3 hours to go – happy!	1m 45s
14	1700	Cup of tea / 3/4 honey sandwich	3m
15	1745	1/4 honey sandwich / 1 bottle carb / chunk energy bar – told to hurry as tide is pushing us down fast!	3m
16	1830	1 bottle carb / 1/4 honey sandwich / very chatty - keen to get on bike!	2m
	1915	FINISH	

Conditions in the Channel

Saturday, 20th September - Supplied by Dover Coast Guard

WMO platform ID: *62304*
Platform name: *Sandettie Lightship*
Position: Latitude 51 ° 6 ' Longitude 1 ° 48 '

Time	Date	Air temp (°C)	Dew point (°C)	Pressure (hPa)	Wind speed (kt)	Wind dir	Max gust (kt)	Sea temp (°C)	Wave height (m)	Wave period (s)	Visibility (km)
05:00	21/09/03	17.95	15.35	1019.4	11.1	NE	*******	18.85	0.30	7.00	20.00
04:00	21/09/03	17.75	16.35	1019.6	12.0	N	*******	18.75	0.30	7.00	4.00
03:00	21/09/03	18.05	16.35	1019.6	8.9	N	*******	18.75	0.20	7.00	4.00
02:00	21/09/03	18.75	13.95	1019.6	14.9	NW	*******	18.75	0.30	7.00	4.00
01:00	21/09/03	18.95	16.55	1019.9	14.0	WNW	*******	18.75	0.30	7.00	4.00
00:00	21/09/03	19.55	16.55	1018.4	12.0	SW	*******	18.75	0.20	7.00	10.00
23:00	20/09/03	19.95	15.45	1018.2	11.1	SSW	*******	18.75	0.30	8.00	10.00
22:00	20/09/03	20.55	14.85	1018.4	13.0	SW	*******	18.75	0.30	7.00	10.00
21:00	20/09/03	20.35	16.65	1018.2	8.9	S	*******	18.75	0.40	7.00	4.00
20:00	20/09/03	19.35	17.95	1018.4	6.0	SE	*******	19.05	0.30	7.00	4.00
19:00	20/09/03	19.45	18.05	1018.2	4.1	ESE	*******	19.25	0.30	7.00	4.00
18:00	20/09/03	19.35	17.95	1018.3	4.1	E	*******	19.25	0.30	7.00	4.00
17:00	20/09/03	19.25	17.55	1018.3	4.1	E	*******	19.35	0.30	7.00	4.00
16:00	20/09/03	19.35	17.45	1018.2	4.1	ENE	*******	19.35	0.30	6.00	4.00
15:00	20/09/03	19.25	17.35	1018.4	6.0	NNE	*******	19.35	0.30	6.00	4.00
14:00	20/09/03	19.25	17.15	1019.3	11.1	NE	*******	19.25	0.20	7.00	4.00
13:00	20/09/03	18.75	16.45	1020.3	8.0	NE	*******	19.15	0.30	6.00	4.00
12:00	20/09/03	18.45	15.95	1020.5	7.0	E	*******	19.15	0.20	7.00	10.00
11:00	20/09/03	17.75	15.25	1020.3	2.9	E	*******	18.95	0.30	6.00	10.00
10:00	20/09/03	17.75	14.75	1021.4	2.9	SSE	*******	18.95	0.20	7.00	10.00
09:00	20/09/03	17.95	15.95	1021.2	1.9	S	*******	18.95	0.30	7.00	4.00
08:00	20/09/03	17.25	14.95	1021.0	2.9	S	*******	18.85	0.30	7.00	4.00
07:00	20/09/03	17.25	14.75	1020.6	4.1	SSW	*******	18.85	0.30	7.00	10.00
06:00	20/09/03	16.95	14.25	1020.0	6.0	WSW	*******	18.85	0.30	8.00	10.00
05:00	20/09/03	16.95	14.15	1020.0	6.0	W	*******	18.85	0.30	7.00	10.00
04:00	20/09/03	16.95	14.35	1019.6	8.0	W	*******	18.95	0.30	6.00	10.00
03:00	20/09/03	17.15	14.05	1019.8	46.0	W	*******	18.85	0.30	6.00	10.00
02:00	20/09/03	17.05	13.45	1020.0	6.0	WSW	*******	18.85	0.30	6.00	10.00
01:00	20/09/03	17.45	14.45	1019.6	11.1	WSW	*******	18.95	0.20	5.00	10.00

Swim Chart Saturday, 20th September

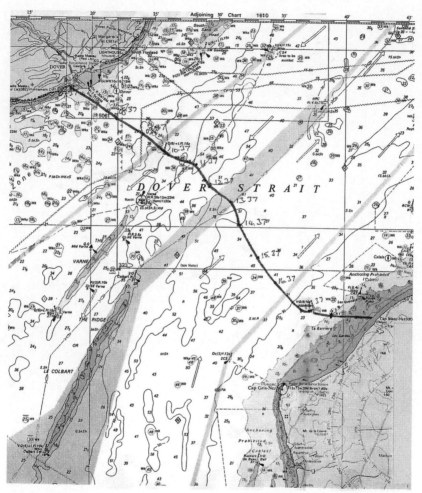

With thanks to Admiralty Leisure.

Me and Mr. Mouncey

For weeks after we returned home we would be amazed at the stories some of our friends told us about where they were and what they were doing as we were ploughing our furrow between London and Paris. This is one such account penned in particular style by The Hairy Hippy for the December edition of the Hinckley Running Club newsletter.

Andy's training took around 4 months. From an initial sea swim of 1 hour he gradually built up to 10 hours in August. This allowed him to get used to cold, the currents and to banish any thoughts of man-eating monsters that may be lurking in the depths. His goal was initially to get to the start line healthy, so not being a natural distance runner he kept his training runs down - the longest being 4 hours - which he did twice and figuring that the bike would (kind of) look after itself. One good thing about spending so much time in cold water was that any niggles picked up were soon sorted out or frozen out to be more precise.

I don't think there have been many times in my life when I dreamt about a man, (well, maybe one other time, Gary Lineker, but I think I was about 8) and it's not something I'd like to make a habit of, I did confess to Niki my wife straight away, but for a few days in September there was a man on my mind, Mr. Mouncey. I'd been telling my family of this chap and his extraordinary challenge for a while, so by September, for some reason I was getting jolly excited. I don't know why. It would be presumptuous of me to say I knew Andy, (although I regularly bellowed at Charlotte on running club nights), but there was something about 'the doing'...not only that but the positive doing. Sounds like something Phil Mitchell might dish out in Eastenders - but you can't help but feel invigorated.

So on September 18th at 12.40 am, Andy got going - looking at the video I could have sworn he nipped off down the tube - a deserted London cheering him off. Unbeknown to everyone else, Andy had set his mind at running the 87 miles. Things started off well enough, 7 mph and reaching Maidstone, 38 miles in 5 hours, then 50 miles inside 8 hours. I guess there aren't many stranger sights than seeing someone receiving massage on a busy roadside.

Watching the pictures you could feel the pain starting to take a grip, (liken it to a cricketer getting one in the bollocks, be male or female, you grimace). And eventually at 70 miles, Andy succumbed to walking. A decision not taken lightly and it meant letting go of the primary goal, (to run the run) and accepting the second one, to finish in one piece. Even though he was walking it was still faster than running, and it looked more comfortable to watch. Having said that, at this point all the downhill bits had to be done backwards as going forwards was too excruciating! But by 7pm and 18 ½ hours later the run was done!

So I was excited and a tad frustrated. I toyed with a trip to London to cheer him off, but I talked myself out of it, and I couldn't wait for progress reports via email from our club secretary, so I learned to text. Previous encounters between me and my mobile had been brief affairs - we've had it years and I've used it about as much as a visiting comet. Still, needs must... the mobile became my new best friend. The first text took a while, but I didn't know text language either, (surprise, surprise) so what could have been sonnet length, in fact turned into a small novel. But hey ho, it got there and bloody hell - I managed to access the reply too. I was cooking!

The next day brought good and bad news. Good that he could move, bad that the swim was postponed. Sunny and calm in Dover doesn't necessarily mean the same in the Channel. 'Twas the same on Thursday and Friday. As Charlotte explained, it wasn't a case of waking up in the morning and having the swim postponed, it was every 6 hours or so. This meant raising your hopes and readying your mind, then having them squished. With delays went any hope of the World Record. Once again the focus had switched to aim for the best split times instead. Dawn on Saturday came and once again the forecast was none too convincing. Predictions of Force 4-6 and the possibility of being pulled from the sea and not completing. The trainer isn't happy, but the boatman is optimistic, it's Andy's call. What's that song about pressure? 'Pressure down on me, pressure down on you, UNDER PRESSURE....' And on top of everything else! Watching the pictures you can almost see it seeping out of Andy. He decides to go. Then came the reward. The Channel behaves like it's had the life sucked out of it, and it's flatter than the flattest supermodel's chest! Never wanting to fully believe their luck, Andy and crew always expect it to turn but it never does. It was the perfect crossing, one little jitter, but a change to the sunny side, and sticking yer woman on the bow solved that. 12 hours and 40 minutes and a sprint finish to the beach. As my ole Ma used to say, 'Jeez baby, yer makes yer luck, yer do!'

It's Saturday and I wonder where he is. A text from Charlotte has raised the possibility of an early start. Late night 'twas the night I dreamt of him. I woke in the morning and lay in bed all snug and warm and pondered the fact that at this very moment Andy could be swallowing the Channel for breakfast. It was a sobering thought, but I soon got over it and had some Cornflakes. Then at 1.30 p.m my friend beeped.

'In the French half of the Channel, lovely for those on the boat.'

Oh joyous! Then later at 5.18 pm...

'The cliffs are in sight.'

This confused me slightly as I thought he might have gone in one big circle and was looking at Dover, but I need not have worried as at 7.43 pm, my beeping beauty once more:

'He's done it. Very happy boy and team.'

I think that summed it up nicely. I sent a text back asking if I could un-cross my testicles now, as I had them crossed since Friday.

Watching the bike leg on the video was funny really, because you knew that Charlotte, Andy and the team knew that they had done it. As Andy said, crossing the Channel was the big one and barring Hurricane Annie, they knew he could do the bike. Having said that it was hot - very hot. The road was long and straight which encouraged Andy to push a bit too hard at the start. This rather took it's toll both mentally and physically and things slowed up, until that was, the fast roads in Paris were hit. In his mind's eye, Andy said he imagined bombing down the Champs Elysée with the Arc d'Triomphe beckoning him on. Unfortunately, the reality was somewhat different as the team hadn't reckoned on (a) half of Paris trying to get home, (b) getting lost, and (c) some French copper almost arresting Andy for trying to cycle up to the Arc. In the end, the end came, and it came with tears of joy, and as I watched Charlotte and Andy's presentation finish there was a little pause - those tears of joy weren't far away again.

Sunday. And before you ask, no I didn't. Got up, went running and was greeted with news of another message:

'Started the bike leg at 6.31 am after a well-deserved kip - Andy is busy trying out his French on Sunday club riders.'

As I lay in the bath soaking my pains away I thought of how much his legs must be aching. It must be purgatory. More texts came in.

'Andy just had 100 mile food stop. 6 hrs 43. Really hot but going steady.'

This was good news indeed and as we sat down for our Sunday lunch we all raised a carrot to Andy's success. It was team time when we heard he had done it. We clinked out tea cups together for a toast, and perhaps for the 35*th* time I explained to Reuben my son what the Arc d'Triomphe was. Personally, I always knew Andy would do it, dunno why, I couldn't explain it either. But I just knew. Many, many congratulations Andy from all at Hinckley Running Club.

Reproduced here with kind permission from Rob Hall-McNair.
(*The Hairy Hippie*)

Arch to Arc by Text

Andy left Marble arch at 0.40am now running SE, beautiful night

Date & Time: 17/09/2003 09:05:02   From:Gemma

Fab hope everything goes well! Every one here is thinking of him! Gem

Date & Time: 17/09/2003 09:27:10   From:Rachel

wish him all the best from the both of us and keep us posted if its possible.thanks rach and mick.

Andy successfully ran through 50 miles by 10.00am well over half the run done

Date & Time: 17/09/2003 10:34:59   From:Kate

I'm amazing my friends with andy's challenge- wow! Sounds like he's doing great

Date & Time: 17/09/2003 10:36:18   From:Gemma

Fantastic bet he is looking great 2. Tell him we r all v excited! Gx

Date & Time: 17/09/2003 17:19:27   From:Steve

Good luck Andy! You're bonkers but I'm proud of you mate. Best of luck for the swim tomorrow. Steve

Date & Time: 17/09/2003 19:02:14   From:Linda

Fantastic news, hope the first bits over with now. nice rest + just a little swim next. well done, lots of luck, were thinking of you linda + rich x x

Andy arrived Dover 7.10pm! Phase one down – bring on the swim – est dep midday

Date & Time: 17/09/2003 19:33:03   From:Sylvie

Fantastic! So impressive! Hope Andy rests well. Thinking of you loads! Allez English bloke! X

Date & Time: 17/09/2003 19:37:36   From:Simon

Wise words from miles, the blind adventurer , "every step and every stroke really counts

Date & Time: 17/09/2003 19:53:3   From:Pattie

Hope u r ok. Have a good rest!

Date & Time: 17/09/2003 22:16:38   From:Rachel

tell andy the best of luck for the swim we've got every confidence in him and we're thinking of him all the way. rach and mick.

Date & Time: 18/09/2003 08:36:43   From:Jim

Hope u slept well + legs not too achy-lindy says go be a dolphin!

Date & Time: 18/09/2003 10:32:49   From:Rob

WELL RUN MR M LOVE PEACE AND FLOWER POWER FOR THE SWIM THE HAIRY HIPPIE CLAN

Date & Time: 18/09/2003 11:38:20   From:Linda

Good luck for the swim. hope conditions are good + you are in good spirit + health linda x

Date & Time: 18/09/2003 11:56:45   From:Kate

Good luck 4 your swim andy! Kate.

Date & Time: 18/09/2003 12:11:29   From:Leyshon

Great run! Have a good swim. Leyshon

Latest Arch to Arc Andy swim delayed due to weather, possible swim start 4.00am fri to be confirmed...

Date & Time: 18/09/2003 12:35:02   From:Steve

Boo to the weather! I hope things clear up for you. Steve

Date & Time: 18/09/2003 12:44:07   From:Gemma

Sorry about that but still have our fingers crossed! X

Date & Time: 18/09/2003 17:02:11   From:Keith

Thanks keep in touch knm

Date & Time: 18/09/2003 18:05:46   From:Philippa

Ok, wIll keep my fingers crossed!

Date & Time: 18/09/2003 20:14:18   From:Keith

Thanks again knm

Date & Time: 18/09/2003 20:49:39   From:Rob

HOWS YER MAN DOIN CHARLOTTE GIVE HIM OUR LOVE HIPPY FAMILY

Arch to Arc update – Still too rough to swim, 4.00am swim off – next opportunity 4.00pm Fri...TBC!

Date & Time: 18/09/2003 23:43:59   From:Gemma

Thanks 4 the update and the waiting must b hard. Everyone still thinking about u both. Gx

Date & Time: 18/09/2003 23:46:49   From:Ian

Come on andy. Come on michael fish.

Date & Time: 19/09/2003 06:46:38   From:Nik

We are thinking of you and hoping for a smooth crossing. Love to you both TIM & NIK

Date & Time: 19/09/2003 07:23:00   From:Jim

Bugger!! How u all feeling? We're thinking of u. Jabba + Jim

Date & Time: 19/09/2003 08:08:03   From:Keith

Thanks enjoy the rest love knm

Date & Time: 19/09/2003 09:00:37   From:Philippa

How's andy doing? Hope he's not getting too fed up waiting. safety is more important. Keep focused. Ps all of oz know what he's up to and ask for updates!

Date & Time: 19/09/2003 11:40:47   From:Rob

HOW SODDING ANNOYINGFOR YOU ALL FINGERS TOES AND TESTICLES CROSSED FOR 4 U

Arch update – still waiting in Dover! New swim start 6.00am Saturday – and this one looks for real! Let's get it on!

Date & Time: 19/09/2003 14:23:04   From:Steve

Hope so - time's ticking by... how are you filling your time?!

Date & Time: 19/09/2003 14:23:38   From:Gemma

Great! Will b waiting 2 hear! Gx

Date & Time: 19/09/2003 14:32:43   From:Ian

Try spinach!

Date & Time: 19/09/2003 16:20:31   From:Dave

HAVE A REST, GET A RUB, FEED YOUR FACE, AND GO FOR IT. Dave.

Date & Time: 19/09/2003 17:19:58   From:Linda

Go for it andy! keep your spirits high (not the alcoholic ones!) best of luck love linda + rich x

Date & Time: 19/09/2003 23:46:19   From:Sylvie

Hello! Thinking of you! Hope Andy can go 4 it Tomorrow. Bon courage et bonne chance! X

Arch to Arc update very tough call this morning – weather still not perfect but Andy choose to go… Started Shakespeare Beach 6.37am

Date & Time: 20/09/2003 07:01:33   From:Lynn

Good luck andy,thinking of u.

Date & Time: 20/09/2003 07:05:36   From:Helen

ALL THE BEST LUV H B

Date & Time: 20/09/2003 07:08:54   From:Penny

We all have our fingers crossed for u both hoping that conditions don't make things 2 difficult during crossing. Good luck again.Pen & Dave xx

Date & Time: 20/09/2003 07:11:17   From:John

Good luck, my thoughts are with you all. Tell him its a walk in the park compared 2 the run ! I hope he put vasalene on his feet, we dont want blisters lol. Tell tim 2 get some good action shots of the 40 foot waves. may the force b with you ! Luv jw x

Date & Time: 20/09/2003 07:59:56   From:Leyshon

Good morning team. Best of luck with crossing. Leyshon.

Date & Time: 20/09/2003 08:09:52   From:Jim

Guess when u get that close u have 2 give it a go. We will keep phone on thinkin of u. Jabba and jin

Date & Time: 20/09/2003 08:45:22   From:Rob

BRILL NEWS CHARLOTTE URGE HIM ON FROM US REMEMBER FLOWER POWER RULS OK GO ANDY GO

Date & Time: 20/09/2003 09:56:01   From:Linda

Hope its going well + its not too rough - the pool this am was bad enough for me! thinking of you both linda x

Date & Time: 20/09/2003 10:27:44   From:Philippa

How is it going - has swim started yet?

Arch to Arc – 1.30pm Andy into the French half of the channel all going good for early eve finish if weather stays good... It's lovely for us on the boat!

Date & Time: 20/09/2003 13:45:05   From:Linda

Thats great news fingers crossed the weather stays good. linda x

Date & Time: 20/09/2003 13:46:20   From:Rachel

We're just heading back from our holiday we'll look out the plane window see if we can spot him! give him our best and we're rooting for him all the way rach and mick.

Date & Time: 20/09/2003 13:46:43   From:Leyshon

Stuck in traffic on m54 , andy moving quicker. Leyshon.

Date & Time: 20/09/2003 13:48:32   From:Jim

Abit like morning sickness! Good to hear so far so good. Allez pour france. Bath duo

Date & Time: 20/09/2003 14:16:27   From:Sylvie

Fantastic! Hope Andy is feeling Ok. French side. .. Allez Andy Allez Andy Allez Andy! X

Date & Time: 20/09/2003 14:25:26   From:Penny

Brilliant news.Look 4wd 2 hearing Andy's   on French soil! P&D x

Date & Time: 20/09/2003 14:33:55   From:Steve

Eddie, Charlotte mes amis, as u r now on the French side of la manche, est-ce que vous parlez en francais. Steve

Date & Time: 20/09/2003 14:52:48   From:Rob

BLOODY BRILL WATCH OUTFOR SUNBURN ON THAT BOAT WISH ANDY WELL

Date & Time: 20/09/2003 15:02:16   From:Lynn

Nice 2 hear things r going good we,ve just had alovely swim not as long as andy!

Date & Time: 20/09/2003 17:16:41   From:Steve

Charlotte, how is Andy holding up ? Steve

Date & Time: 20/09/2003 17:20:42   From:Simon

Keep going!!

Arch to Arc latest – Andy has the cliffs in sight! Estimate appeox 7.30pm landing

Date & Time: 20/09/2003 17:23:59   From:Dave

WHEN HE COMES UP FOR AIR TELL HIM TO KEEP UP THE GOOD WORK, + TELL HIM NOT TO TRY TO SPRINT UP THE BEACH ! Dave(massage)

Date & Time: 20/09/2003 17:24:09   From:Tim

Fantastic! Give him a shout from me and cath, tim puffer

Date & Time: 20/09/2003 17:27:06   From:Linda

Fantastic!! i bet andy's pleased the end of the swim is in sight! linda x

Date & Time: 20/09/2003 17:28:28   From:Penny

Fantastic news.Have just been 2 church 2 c Keith&Jen-they looked fab-off 2 reception at 7.30 so will think of u & update the HRC crew.Hp Bike goes well.Pen x

Date & Time: 20/09/2003 17:30:11   From:Keith

Great news keep it up love knm

Date & Time: 20/09/2003 17:35:14   From:Jim

Wow! Allez andy, allez andy - not far now - keep eating the jelly babies! Reynolds rec.

Date & Time: 20/09/2003 17:35:41   From:Helen

WONDERFUL LUV H AND B

Date & Time: 20/09/2003 17:39:04   From:Nik

Go ANDY! all at the wedding are following progress with hearts in mouth, he is in the speech!

Date & Time: 20/09/2003 18:30:20   From:Rob

GGGOOO GO MR M BILLY WHIZZ IN A WETSUIT YOU BEAUTY FLOWER POWER 4EVER

Date & Time: 20/09/2003 18:34:06   From:Kate

Go andy! How far is the challenge altogether, we have been discussing it. Wedding's gone real well and everyone wishes andy well. U missed out on profiteroles!

He's done it! 12hrs 38mins phase 2 down!! A very happy boy & team!

Date & Time: 20/09/2003 19:44:25   From:Dave

CONGRAT'S MATE GREAT ACHIEVEMENT. SLEEP WELL. Dave(massage)

Date & Time: 20/09/2003 19:44:45   From:Kate

Jon and tim said that's a bit slow! Well done mate! X

Date & Time: 20/09/2003 19:45:39   From:Malc

FANTASTIC I WAS JUST ABOUT TO TEXT U MANY MANY CONGRATULATIONS COME TO TENERIFE TO CELEBRATE

Date & Time: 20/09/2003 19:47:02   From:Jim

Absolutely brill-boy done good! Thrilled here 2, j+j

Date & Time: 20/09/2003 19:49:01   From:Steve

Fantastic! Best of luck for a puncture-free home run!

Date & Time: 20/09/2003 19:49:42   From:Mike

Fantastic. We're so excited. Brilliant achievent. Mike and Jo.

Date & Time: 20/09/2003 19:51:20   From:Simon

Amazing well done all of you   roll on Paris

Date & Time: 20/09/2003 19:51:26   From:Rob

YYYYYYEEEEESSS MANY MANY CONGRATULATIONS TO YOU ALL ABSOLUTLEY MAGIC

Date & Time: 20/09/2003 19:51:46   From:Tim

Fantastic, 'much respect', well done to all. Tim and cath puffer.

Date & Time: 20/09/2003 19:54:05   From:Pattie

Well done, very pleased 4 u all!

Date & Time: 20/09/2003 20:11:57   From:Sylvie

Well Done! Have a good rest! Andy you must so proud & .... knackered! The others you must b relieved! R u on track for a Record ? Lots of love and kisses S

Date & Time: 20/09/2003 20:12:20   From:Rachel

thats brilliant news and a quick crossing although andy probably doesnt think so.tell him well done and good luck for the home straight!

Date & Time: 20/09/2003 20:18:10   From:John

well done .great news. easy bit left to do...Madrid is hot& dusty. Back Monday. Will ring.

Date & Time: 20/09/2003 20:28:22   From:Helen

5 ?CONGRATS H AND A*AA SORRY B

Date & Time: 20/09/2003 20:32:32   From:Lynn

Still having trouble with phone hows the swimmer? No wetsuit next time!

Date & Time: 20/09/2003 21:04:29   From:Keith

Excellent news were very happy too all the best for the last lap loveknm

Date & Time: 20/09/2003 23:06:52   From:Ian

Mouncey the magnificent! Come on andy! Watch out for speed cameras.

Date & Time: 20/09/2003 23:53:06   From:Penny

Fantastic!Well done that man!Cycling should be down hill?!!?Thinking of u both.Love Pen&Dave x

Date & Time: 21/09/2003 01:20:55   From:Gemma

Wow! What a high nearly there! Gx

> **Arch to Arc – Andy started bike leg at 6.31am French time, after well deserved kip! He is busy trying his French on Sunday club riders!**

Date & Time: 21/09/2003 07:52:10   From:Jon

Excellent! Enjoy ride into paris

Date & Time: 21/09/2003 08:08:17   From:Leyshon

Good morning all . Impressed!, off to do bala tri. Leyshon& ray.

Date & Time: 21/09/2003 08:42:57   From:Philippa

Well done. That is the hard bit done - it is all down hill from here! Go andy go!

Date & Time: 21/09/2003 08:48:14   From:Penny

Hope the cycling continues 2 go well.We're off 2 do Wolvey 10m-insignificant after Andy's exploits! but thinking of u both.A bientot!Pen&Dave x

Date & Time: 21/09/2003 09:08:48   From:Jim

Hope the french he knows is clean! Both of us r so chuffed and quite emotional and wish we could b there. Could u do live cnverage next year! Spk 2 u soon l + j

Date & Time: 21/09/2003 09:25:49   From:Tim

Next stop Paris! What a man! Oh and wife.

Date & Time: 21/09/2003 09:58:51   From:Helen

THIS IS WEARING US OUT LUV H AND B

Date & Time: 21/09/2003 10:25:47   From:Sylvie

Bonjour! Et bonne route! A plus tard!

Date & Time: 21/09/2003 10:44:22   From:Jenni

Thanks for your thoughts, card & vouchers. Had a fab day. Hope all is still going well & we'll look forward to seeing you both soon. Love Jen & Keith

Date & Time: 21/09/2003 10:47:44   From:Steve

immense interest in britain and america interview arranged for american mag

> **Arch to Arc – Andy just had a 100 mile food stop. 6hrs 43mins from the start – 80ish miles to go! Really hot again but he's going steady**

Date & Time: 21/09/2003 13:20:43   From:Jim

Jims over half way with cutting the hedge im supporting were havin an action packed day! Gettin all the jobs done before wedsnd.j+l

Date & Time: 21/09/2003 13:22:19   From:Rob

LE MAGNIFIC WE WILL RAISE A CARROT AND ROASTIE IN ANDYS HONOUR

Date & Time: 21/09/2003 13:52:15   From:Tim

Brill, he's my main man now, give him a shout for me please charley. Tim x

Date & Time: 21/09/2003 14:40:19   From:Sylvie

All my thoughts go 2 Andy. Good 2 have updates! Allez english bloke! X

Date & Time: 21/09/2003 14:40:57   From:Penny

You must be feeling so excited-& relieved that Andy's on last leg.Enjoy the triumph at the Arc de Triumph!Pen & Dave x

Date & Time: 21/09/2003 14:56:11   From:Dave

KEEP GOING MATE NEARLY THERE. Dave(massage)

Date & Time: 21/09/2003 15:12:43   From:Linda

Absolutely fantastic!! i have just done 70 on the bike + am dead now! just absolutely amazing - what a stuning performance + the end in sight what a guy! Linda

Date & Time: 21/09/2003 16:59:40   From:Lynn

Hi how r things going?

Date & Time: 21/09/2003 17:12:15   From:Lynn

I am so pleased andy has done so well.wendy and me r so jealous of his time 4 the swim!what did he have 4 his breakfast that day?because we want some! not long 2 go.will wait 4 the next text 2 say he has finished!luv 2 ed as well

Date & Time: 21/09/2003 20:01:24   From:Lynn

Whats happening!has he got there?

Arch to Arc – we're here!! Andy has cracked it – details to follow!

Date & Time: 21/09/2003 20:14:21   From:Jenni

CONGRATULATIONS!!!

Date & Time: 21/09/2003 20:15:15   From:Malc

AN AMAZING ACHIEVEMENT CONGRATS TO YOU BOTH HAUE JUST RESERVED 2 TICKETS ON TUESDAY EVENING TO JOIN US NO COST FLYING BACK 3 OCT LOTS TO DISCUSS AND CBRATE

Date & Time: 21/09/2003 20:18:24   From:Leyshon

Well done from leyshon & ray. still in traffiç jam

Date & Time: 21/09/2003 20:18:31   From:Rachel

nice one and massive congratulations from the both of us! we'll be in touch real soon!

Date & Time: 21/09/2003 20:19:15   From:Mike

Congratulations. We've loved sharing it with you. Jo and Mike

Date & Time: 21/09/2003 20:20:10   From:Pattie

A very big well done!!

Date & Time: 21/09/2003 20:20:27   From:Gemma

Fantastic! Bet u r all high as kites! Enjoy Paris. Gem

Date & Time: 21/09/2003 20:23:05   From:Lynn

Hooray!well done everyone!

Date & Time: 21/09/2003 20:24:23   From:Steve

Magnifique! Fantastique!! and other French superlatives to all of you - a real team effort. And hats off to Andy - if he was bouncy before he'll be boingey now!

Date & Time: 21/09/2003 20:32:41   From:Rob

ABSOLUTLEY MAGIC WELL DONE TO YOU ALL CAN IKNOW UNCROSS MY TESTICLES

Date & Time: 21/09/2003 20:35:29   From:Ian

Congratulations! Incredible! What a star. We salute u.

Date & Time: 21/09/2003 20:45:45   From:Nik

We are really proud and trilled for you both love Tim & Nik

Date & Time: 21/09/2003 20:51:37   From:Dave

WELL DONE ANDY, GREAT STUFF. SPEAK TO YOU SOON. Dave.

Date & Time: 21/09/2003 21:03:06   From:Anne

Huge congratulations and much respect . Tell andy to remember to get in the van on the way home!

Date & Time: 21/09/2003 21:17:22   From:Penny

Fantastic achievement!(dave says he'll excuse u from Tues speed work!)Look 4wd 2 hearing details when u r back on English soil.Pen & Dave x

Date & Time: 21/09/2003 21:18:28   From:Simon

Amazing! A truly insipational accomplishment well done mate and to all of you that made it possible. Let me know if there is anything i can do to spread the word

Date & Time: 21/09/2003 21:40:53   From:Tim

Congratulations to u all. What a result! Tim Puffer.

Date & Time: 21/09/2003 21:48:28   From:Steve

Wonderful, fantasticaly well done to Andy & ALL of you.

Date & Time: 21/09/2003 22:03:05   From:Sylvie

What can I say... Fantastically well done! Looking forward to hear all about it in person. Let me know when you're home. Sx

Date & Time: 21/09/2003 22:22:16   From:Keith

Congratulations what a splendid achievement love knm

Date & Time: 21/09/2003 22:29:48   From:Linda

Thats fantastic news + an incredible feat of endurance. we are both so pleased + full of admiration for what you have done. have a great evening rich + lindax

ENDUROMAN Arch to arc roundup – Run split 87m in 18hrs 30mins, Channel swim 12hrs 38mins, Bike split 180m 14hrs 17mins – new fastest splits, but total time 115hrs 8mins

Date & Time: 22/09/2003 08:28:48   From:John

Congrats 2 the big man and the team. Well done ! Jw

Date & Time: 22/09/2003 08:52:47   From:Steve

Fantastic achievement. Enjoy Paris. Steve

Date & Time: 22/09/2003 08:56:38   From:Sylvie

Well how impressive are those results?! Hope Andy is not 2 wound up with the 8 mn. Take care. Sylvie

Date & Time: 22/09/2003 08:56:43   From:Tim

Never mind our support your the one thats awesome mate. Well done. Tim -Cath Puffer

Date & Time: 22/09/2003 09:09:56   From:Malc

AN AMAZING ACHIEVEMENT CONGRATS TO YOU BOTH HAUE JUST RESERVED 2 TICKETS ON TUESDAY EVENING TO JOIN US NO COST FLYING BACK 3 OCT LOTS TO DISCUSS AND CBRATE

Date & Time: 22/09/2003 09:41:41   From:Lynn

He should b very pleased with himself! Whats next? I still want 2 know what he had 4 his breakfast the day of his swim! Was it baked beans!

Date & Time: 22/09/2003 10:24:50   From:Jon

Fantastic achievement!! Well done jb

Andy set to travel from Arch to Arc

By Mark McGlynn

IN these days of the Eurostar rail service, travellers can be in ... within about three hours ... ... relax- ...

then cycling the remaining 180 miles from Calais into the centre

sheer monotony of having lit... no sensory stimulat... but a few ...

3, 2003

EVENING TELEGRAPH

Ironman set for Arch to Arc bid

By SIMON DUDMAN

TRIATHLETE Andy Mouncey hopes to become only the second person to ... from London to ...

graduate, 36, will be attempting the Arch to Arc Challenge, between ... the Arch in London ... Triomphe

a punishing 16-week training programme.

He will be following in the footsteps of ironman and outdoor sports specialist Eddie Ette, who completed the 289-mile challenge in 80hr 5min ... 2001.

Andy, who lives in Stoney Stanton, near Hinckley, runs his own personal coaching business, called the Coach Company, and has coached swimmers in Coventry such as Commonwealth gold medalist Adam Whitehead and British record holder

---

ARCH TO ARC IN 80 HOURS?

GET fit for Life lecturer Andy Mouncey is on countdown to an incredible London to Paris challenge.

By ZOE ASHTON

Triathlete Andy, 36, who has been taking seminars for the distance learning course at Rugby College, will be running the 87 miles from London's Marble Arch to Dover, swimming 22 miles across the Channel and then cycling the 180 miles from Calais to l'Arc de Triomphe in Paris.

The only other person to do this was Eddie Ette in 2001 and Andy is going to beat his 80-hour time and earn a place in the Guinness Book of ...

...die is helping Andy to train for ... challenge due to take place ... September 17-23.

...dy explained: "In my work as a ...al coach, whoever I am help-... common denominator is just ... the confidence to face some-... which looks pretty big and ...

... personal challenge is a ... people's attention ... I am and what I ...

... bid for Andy ... while he has ... the sea in ... ... ing could ... and 15 ...

though I wear a wetsuit it's still cold," he said.

"I try and get into a mental state which athletes call 'in the zone'. That's where I'm very closely aware

of the technical aspects of what I'm doing, but my mind is somewhere else and I'm not conscious of the hours passing.

Along the way Andy, from Leicestershire, will be treading water every 35 minutes to take on food and water. Most of his calories will come from liquid carbohydrate drinks but he has been experimenting with other ...

"I need a variety, so I've been try...

...ing malt loaf, tinned fruit cocktail, energy bars, bananas and reward foods like jaffa cakes and jelly babies. I need to eat quickly because when you stop you cool down.

Andy feels the run is the next most important element of the challenge and the cycling the least, because once he's in France all he has to do is stay on the bike!

"I'd be lying to say the record is an issue," he added. "But as people in my job, I've see many different goals, so I have elements of motivat... have one book that w... disappeared ...

"The challenge is ... nal. Of course ther... preparation, but ... straightforward ...

"Like anyon... your skills fro... day, the onl... good day w... and a bad d... what's goin...

... £5,000 ... nesses ... his life ... He ... he bli...

Andy Mouncey breaks for a drink during a training swim

Businessman is training for the ultimate challenge

In the swim with a marathon effort

by **Ellie Pio**
News Report

Eddie gave me was 'just get your
and swim'. The thing

FOR most pe
narathon w
llenge. I

Athlete Andy proves he's the fastest mover

BY FRANCESCA WINRO

Swimming the English
Channel would be a
daunting enough challenge
for anyone.

But not for 56-year-old Sup-
cote triathlete Andy Mouncey. He completed an 87-
run before reach-
water's edge
had finis
went

to swim the
Channel i
ished u
180-mile
fle

L█ARCH TO ARC
█ndon : Dover : Calais : Paris

'Superman' Andy goes down in history

Picture by **Tim Jury**

by **Ellie Piovesana**
News Reporter

A TAMWORTH coach has
proved he can 'walk the
walk' by running the equi-
alent of three marathons.
imming the 180 miles across
Mouncey com-
cult chal-
wn in

But the hardest task was still to
come. After waiting for two day.
for good weather, Andy had to
make a decision, swim now or call
the whole thing off.
   "That was one of the hardest
moments," he remembers. "The
only thing that could have
stopped me was the weather. I
decided that if they had to pull me
out the water I could at least walk
away and say I tried my best."
   Luckily for Andy the weather
held out and he made it across in
12 hours – five hours quicker than
Eddie.
   At 5.30am the next morning, Andy
just four hours sleep, Andy
is bike and cycled 180
down steep hills in

SPORT

e were a
title

The biggest, scariest challenge yet

ANDY Mouncey's amaz-
ing triathlon took him
all the way from

By **ZOE ASHTON**

Sportsdesk Tel: 01788 539975
THURSDAY, OCTOBER 2, 2003

wards down hills,

More About The Author

After some 10 years working in the health and fitness industry, Andy formed his own Performance Coaching business in 2001. The Coach Company helps people from all walks of life to Find Their Sparkle! - and we all know people who sparkle, don't we? - and to achieve their own Big & Scary! challenges, be that in sport, education, business or everyday life.

Performance Is Emotional

The physical preparation for the Enduroman Arch to Arc Challenge was relatively straightforward, but the key to consistent High Performance was in preparing the mind. This was the real hard part, and Andy learned that for him, what this actually came down to was six simple steps.

The Doing Big & Scary! material - whether that be coaching, presenting or workshops - uses stories from the Challenge to illustrate how these Six Steps actually worked - and how they could work for you in your own performance environment in your sport, school or college, at work or at home.

As a Performance Coach and Inspirational Speaker, Andy continues to work with people in business, sport, education and everyday life. While the range in the client base is a feature of The Coach Company, Andy retains a sports performance specialism and has helped athletes to British, Commonwealth, and European titles and the Irish Olympic Team for Athens 2004.

Some of the organisations Andy has worked with include:
- Institute of Directors
- AstraZeneca, Sweden
- BBC Radio Leicester
- British Triathlon Association
- West Leicestershire Mind - The Mental Health Charity
- Nat West Bank
- The City of Coventry Swimming Club
- Zurich Advice Network
- Coventry University
- Business Link
- Leicestershire Education & Business Company

Available in the Doing Big & Scary! series:

Audio CD of the Doing Big & Scary! Presentation. 80 minutes of Andy in conversation with the Six Step Guide from the story of his Enduroman Arch to Arch Challenge.

Doing Big & Scary! Presentation Workbook. A transcript of the audio CD including the Key Learns and exercises for you to complete.

A Book of Advice. Copies of the book made for Andy by primary school children.

Audio CDs in the Six Step Series. Andy talks you through the application of each of the Six Steps in turn.

Step 1: Goals To Really Grab You.
Step 2: Create Team Me
Step 3: Keep It Simple
Step 4: Focus On What You Can Control
Step 5: Rest, Reflect and Recuperate
Step 6: Smile, Celebrate and Re-Set The Goal

Buy on line at www.coachco.co.uk
andy@coachco.co.uk

For more information about the Enduroman
Arch to Arc Challenge
Contact Eddie Ette at:

www.enduroman.com